FLIGHT TO FREEDOM

God's Faithfulness in Communist Romania

by
ELENA RĂSCOL-RADY

FLIGHT TO FREEDOM
God's Faithfulness in Communist Romania

by

ELENA RĂSCOL-RADY

All Rights Reserved
© 2015

ISBN-13: 978-1511575270
ISBN-10: 1511575271

All Scriptures are taken from the Authorized King James Version

All rights reserved, including the right to reproduce this book, or any portions thereof, in any form. No part of this book may be reproduced or transmitted in any form or by any means without written permission from ELENA RĂSCOL-RADY All rights for publishing this book or portions thereof in other languages are contracted by the author.

Contents

Foreword v
Romanian Editor's Note vii
Prelude xi
Author's Note xv

~ PART ONE ~
Prelude to Destiny 1

~ PART TWO ~
All Grown Up 13

~ PART THREE ~
Learning Endurance 31

~ PART FOUR ~
True Love 57

~ PART FIVE ~
Complications 75

~PART SIX~
Smuggling and Singing 95

~ PART SEVEN ~
Crossing Boarders 117

~ PART EIGHT ~
Lessons in Faith 143

~ PART NINE ~
Freedom's Promise 165

~ PART TEN ~
Together at Last 183
Appendix 1 205
Appendix 2 213

FLIGHT TO FREEDOM

Foreword

I have known Vasile and Elena (or "Puşa", as her close friends used to call her) since I was young, and I enjoyed wonderful times of fellowship with their family in church, in their home, and at work (the Agricultural Academy where Vasile and I worked together). If I had to sum up in a nutshell their character and work, the words I would pick would be commitment, integrity, suffering and, with God's help, joy in the victory that followed.

The Apostle Paul wrote to the Philippians: "For to you it has been granted on behalf of Christ, not only to believe in Him, but also to suffer for His sake" (1:29). As St. John Chrysostom says, man is purified and strengthened through suffering, as gold is refined in the smelter.

The reading of this book introduces us to some of God's people who were the history makers of the Protestant churches, such as the Wurmbrands, Caraman, Ioanid, Boeru, Paul Niculescu, Aurel Popescu and others who have suffered for the faith and for the Lord's work. All of them were close to the Răscol (now known as Răscol-Rady) family, and most of them were my friends as well.

Just like Vasile, these and many others were investigated by the Romanian Secret Police for having preached the gospel of Christ with a sincere heart; for distributing Bibles and religious literature; for their connections with the believers outside Romania; and for the support they offered in various ways to those in need.

Although the Communist Romanian Constitution granted freedom of conscience and this value was theoretically promoted, things were very different in reality.

Abraham Lincoln, once said: "Those who deny freedom to others, deserve it not for themselves; and, under a just God, cannot long retain it."

Only those who have experienced the same trials as this family can understand the torment of being investigated or imprisoned for the faith; tortured in order to reveal the names of other collaborators; treated like a dangerous criminal; being separated from loved ones; and longing to see one's children whose fate was uncertain.

I remember a painful episode Puşa Răscol-Rady went through while her husband was in prison. I happened to arrive at their door while their apartment was being searched by the Secret Police. I had come to help little Dorinel learn German. When I walked in through the open door, I saw three men inside. One of them was taking notes about the search, another one was on the phone and the third one asked me why I was there. "I'm tutoring the boy," I replied.

That same moment the agent talking on the phone announced to the others, "We're done here. How about you?"

I found out only later that the Secret Police agents had also searched the homes of our brothers Pavel Nicolescu, Caraman, Aurel Popescu and others.

After they left, Puşa showed me countless letters of sympathy as well as supportive messages from senators and members of the US Congress. News of her husband's arrest had spread all around the world.

"If anyone suffers as a Christian, let him not be ashamed," writes the Apostle Peter in his first epistle (4:16).

May God bless the Răscol-Radys and reward everything Vasile and Puşa did in His Name.

This book is equally useful for those who have known this family, and for the younger generation that thus will have the opportunity to find out about the times we lived in. May they thank the Lord for the freedom they enjoy today and resolve to get the best out of it.

—Cristian Vasile Roske, *Pastor in Bucharest*

Romanian Editor's Note

*I*met the author of this book quite late, after the events described on its pages, during one of the visits she made in Romania. Although we spent only a short time together, her words stayed with me like a precious memory. However, I didn't know anything about the experiences she had been through in Romania, nor about the reasons that forced her out of her the homeland so dear to her. I understood all these only when I read this book of remembrance. The writer's pure love for her Savior and sincere commitment to Him touched me deeply. Reading page after page, I followed in her footsteps and saw the rough path she was destined to walk. I felt her pain when her father was imprisoned, and in my mind journeyed next to her in the heat of the dusty roads to the place of his doom.

I also read about her marriage, her father's return, her motherhood, and her family's involvement in the Lord's ministry. Tragedy struck her life again when her husband was imprisoned. This time the pain was much stronger. For six months she had no news about him and she had to raise all by herself two children who kept on asking where their father was. The fight she had to face outside the prison walls was no easier than her husband's. The merciless wave of persecution hit her as well when she had to choose between accepting a decree that required the denial of her faith or rejecting it, and consequently losing her job. This woman had the power to reject the compromise and she stood strong because her roots ran deep in the eternal Rock.

In God's precise timing the prison gate opened again and her husband Vasile returned home. He slowly recovered from the physical and mental suffering he was subject to, but the Secret Police continued to harass both of them, threatening, interrogating and denying them any chance to find a job. However, the heads of the Secret Police didn't know that all their efforts were doomed to absolute failure, because the Most High had decided a long time ago that He would take this family out of their country of origin. God's plan for their life was fulfilled to the letter and they were able to get to the free world not as defeated or desperate people, but as soldiers in the army of the King of kings. Their departure completed the first stage of their ministry. The book ends here and does not record what followed afterwards—a fruitful ministry and a life of whole-hearted commitment.

After reading the life story of this family, with God's help I was able to get beyond the letters on the pages of the book and see the sacred work planned for them by our Lord, who knew them before they were born and who loved them so much that He entrusted them with a very special mission for which He prepared them beforehand. Both Pușa and Vasile were born in very scenic areas of Romania. She grew up on the shores of the Danube River, while he was raised in beautiful Bucovina. The Word of Life was sown early in their hearts and they both had excellent role models in their families. That was a time of great love and unity among believers, and these two were chosen to fulfill a special ministry. Therefore, they had to develop and grow under the toughest "school" of the time—communist persecution. But no weapon used against them could extinguish their love for God, whose fire is even stronger than death. Therefore, their work for the persecuted church in Romania did not end once they left the country, but continued even stronger and more intensely than before.

It was a true blessing for me to know these believers. Both of them impressed me with their simple and open demeanor. Sister Pușa gave me some valuable advice which I could pass on to others. As for Brother Vasile, the gentleness and peace of his face spoke volumes; they did not give away the sufferings he had been through and for which he will be rewarded by the King of life Himself, in the Kingdom of heaven, where he will stay forever with his Lord.

For the new generation, with its tendency to reconcile Christian living with the image of the world, this book is like the trumpet sound of some daring pioneers. Let's pay attention to it! We will be one day in front of God in the presence of such people if we stand our ground till the end.

—Cecilia Molece, *one of the writer's disciples*

x *FLIGHT TO FREEDOM*

PRELUDE

"I have been young, and now am old; yet have I not seen the righteous forsaken, nor his seed begging bread" (Psalm 37:25). This was my father, Gheorghiță Boeru's, favorite Bible verse.

Reading along—or better spoken, devouring—all the lines written by Pușa Răscol, I thought father was right. Or rather, I understood anew the truth of the above-quoted verse, reliving many of the wonderful moments. However, I also felt the heartbeats threatening to engulf me in the uncertainty of the coming years. One of the memories stuck in my mind, as if it happened only yesterday . . .

We were in our home on Poterași Street, where the Ioanids, and Aurel Popescu's family were our neighbors. I include this detail so you the reader can perhaps get a grasp of the warm, brotherly atmosphere surrounding us, as we physically lived in proximity to our brethren. Pușa and Vasile had just come to see us. We were aware of Vasile's being tailed, and were even enjoying some innocent fun, exposing the hiding places of the secret police men, which were somewhat childish, offering little concealment.

I don't know whether the Securitate agents were so dim, or if they didn't care about being discovered. The fact is, from our balcony on the second floor of our apartment I spotted right away a suspicious-looking guy waiting at the corner of the adjacent street. Upon a casual inspection of the street, I soon discovered another one, who openly leaned against the fence of the neighbor's house. At that moment, I suggested to Vasile that we have some fun by making them wait in our area far longer than they had planned. Vasile was surprised at this strange development, but next I showed him another corridor, which led from the kitchen and exited our home onto a different alley. Knowing the proverbial vigilance of the Securitate people, I soon realized they knew nothing of this alternate exit. I had hardly said this, when our visitors decided to leave, using the secret exit from our home. So the Securitate agents kept watching our home until, in the end, they either realized they'd been had (unable to explain this), or they must have got tired of waiting (for it was quite dark by now). So, in the end, they were forced to report to their superiors the failure of their mission.

I remember fondly a little vacation I had in the company of Auntie Alice (who used to live with us) and Dorinel, the son of the Răscols. I was a teenager then, with lots of questions and worries flooding my mind, even for someone who had been raised in a Christian home. However, Auntie Alice (Panaiodor), who did a lot of work with children in Sunday School, gained more experience working with a 14-year old girl and a boy of four. For me it was a wonderful, blessed experience, leading to my conversion to the Lord, even before the graduating ceremony from the eight-year elementary school—which, incidentally, I skipped!

One glorious spring day, as I was drinking in the fragrance of the blossoming trees, gently blowing across my face, I saw a swallow freshly returned from warmer countries. She was "talking" with her friends, trying to win an argument over them. I felt a bit jealous! How wonderful to be a bird! For a few moments I closed my eyes and did a bit of flying with her.

I surveyed the mountains, the sea, the clouds, and the sun, spreading its gentle warmth. Suddenly, right next to me, another little bird was shot by a hunter . . . All I had to do was open my eyes, and the peril would have disappeared . . . Then we rested for a while on a branch. Underneath the children were aiming their slings at us . . . All I had to do was open my eyes, and the peril would have disappeared . . . We flew on, and at the next break, I saw a black cat, seemingly half-famished, circling the twig . . . Once again, all I had to do was open my eyes, and the peril would have disappeared—for me, but not for the bird!

Very soon I realized a bird's life is nothing "to write home about it," for apart from the advantage of flight, my life as a human being does offer me more prospects! But first of all, I understood something else: that in any given circumstance all I have to do is open my eyes, acknowledge

God, and every peril will go away.

It is my firm belief that this is how our fellow believers, who endured all the fiery trials of the communist prisons, have survived: by looking at Jesus, and fixing their eyes on Him.

I think it is of paramount importance today, when these "champions of faith" are increasingly covered by the dust of time, to remind the coming generations of all the glorious wonders God can and does accomplish in the lives of those who trust and witness for Him.

I thank Pușa for this book.

—Gabriela Boeru Ander, *Eschwege / Vinarós*

AUTHOR'S NOTE

In the summer of 2006 I was in Constantza, Romania accompanying our son-in-law, David Copp, the pastor of a church in Long Beach, California. David had been invited by Pastor Ghiță Ritișan to come and address a number of churches in the area, and to teach a seminar for some local pastors in Constantza.

The main topic, *A Truly Christian Life*, attracted many participants because of David's spiritual gift of explaining ideas and communicating clearly.

Often the meetings continued on after the end of the service. Many had questions arising from a deep spiritual thirst and hunger. They desired to learn about the genuine Christian life of the early Church.

In such circumstances, I was often asked to tell of our way of living as Christians in Romania under Communist persecution. I was amazed at their curiosity until they told me plainly:

"You see, we, the new generation, know nothing of your experiences. For us, freedom of belief is something so natural! Unless you, who went through those times, tell us all about it, we will miss the example of how God's Spirit works in the Church under persecution. Should we ever also have to suffer for our faith, your example will greatly help."

Back home in the US, where I have lived since 1978, the Lord allowed us to enjoy fellowship with many Christians, and not a few have asked us to tell them about our lives. Our children and grandchildren wanted to have our experiences stand as A BOOK OF REMEMBRANCE.

The freedom of faith, as we knew it upon arriving in America, is no longer the same, and we can see clearly where we are headed. However, the way of the Lord Jesus is the same. It is a narrow but blessed way. The children of God are awakening to a dimension of true service, getting ready for and hastening the day of the Lord Jesus' Coming.

It is worth living in such a time.

I dedicate what I have written to our children, Dorian and Cristiana, to our grandchildren, Landon, Aaron, Lauren, Selah, Emma, Judah and Bria, and to all those who will read it.

Most of all, I'd like to thank my husband, Vasile Răscol, without whom nothing would have been written.

Please note that Vasile's family name in Romania is Răscol. After we left Communist Romania to live in the West, we changed our name to Rady so that we could travel back to Romania travel back to Romania regularly—bringing material aid to the suffering churches from Christian missions in America—without endangering anyone.

Elena Răscol

~ PART ONE ~

Prelude to Destiny
*The story took place before 1977.
It is the story of my family.*

Looking out the small window of the plane that took us from Bucharest to Paris, I could not hold back my tears. I was leaving my country together with my husband Vasile and our children, Dorian and Cristiana. I saw there, far below, the group of people that had come to bid us goodbye and I felt like a little lamb that had been taken from the flock and sent out into the unknown world. Everything I had known and loved was left behind and was growing smaller and smaller by the minute until it disappeared completely from my sight, but not from my heart.

Through the mist of tears I was not able to see the beautiful clear sky, but only images from my life that seemed to play on the screen of my mind.

Early Childhood

I was born in Galați, a town situated by the banks of the Danube River. My grandfather, Papa Dimache, was a tall, strong, good man, respected by all because he had made his fortune by honest hard

Papa Dimache

work. Though he had only been through primary school he was considered an educated man because he was able to write and to calculate very well. This is how he managed his own money and opened up several businesses.

Dimache and Anghelache

He lived close to the harbor, and all the ships that stopped there went to his shops for supplies. Even the tram station was called "At Dimache".

His only son Anghelache, who was to become my father, got married and had a son of his own, Valentin. The boy's mom died soon after he was born, so Valentin was raised by his grandparents.

Some years later, Papa Dimache noticed a pretty girl who used to come to his stores to buy food quite often. He inquired about her and found out she had been born in Galați but raised in Bucovina, where she had recently returned from. He introduced her to his son, and pretty soon they threw a beautiful, cheerful engagement party, with lots of gifts for the bride-to-be, though his son was 12 years older than his fiancée, who was only 15.

Many girls envied Măndița, the young lady chosen to be Dimache's daughter-in-law, though she was poor.

My father

But Anghelache had his own group of friends he used to spend his time and have fun with, so he rarely thought about his fiancée. Therefore one day she took all the gifts she had received at the engagement party and returned them to her fiancé's father. She didn't want his money, but a husband who would love and respect her. Once she called off the engagement, her former fiancé carried on with his cheerful life and she went back to school. She graduated, got her diploma as a radiology technician, and got a job at a hospital in Galați. She was no longer the naïve girl from the countryside but a beautiful and educated young woman.

Sometime later my father happened to meet her again and fall in love with her for the first time. My mother had loved him from the very beginning and she still had feelings for him.

They got married and I was born one year later. They named me Elena but called me Pușa, a common nickname for a little girl. I already had a brother (Valentin) who was 8 years older than me.

Mom and Dad at Their Wedding

A few years after WW2, my parents decided to start a new life on their own, separating themselves from my grandparents. I was six when we moved to Bucharest. Valentin stayed for a while with my grandparents.

There in the capital, my parents found a restaurant they wanted to run. Restaurant is actually too fancy a word, because the place was more of a pub. With the help of my grandparents from my mother's side, my parents were able to make it. They worked from dusk to dawn, and had to pay rent to the landlord as well. He lived in a room in the same building. I spent most of the day there too, until my parents would take me home at night half asleep.

We lived in two rooms situated in a small building, but we had a large inner court that we shared with all the tenants in the many small, old buildings around it. We rented that place "temporarily", hoping we

My mom and me

Me, Mom and Valentin

Me at the end of the school year

would find a better one later. However there is nothing more permanent than the temporary. At least that was our experience, caused by circumstances nobody expected back then.

I was six when I started going to school. When the classes were over I used to play outside. When the weather was nice I played hopscotch on the sidewalk, and in wintertime I would go sleighing.

In bad weather I would stay in the

landlord's room, often falling asleep there in spite of the noise and crude yelling of the drunken customers. I was doing pretty well in school, especially after Valentin joined us. He was a very smart boy and used to help me with my homework. I was so fond of him.

Communism Is Coming

All the people around us were hoping that better times were ahead. But those times did not come. Communism appeared on the scene instead. What could a child of my age understand about the new regime? I only understood we no longer had a king. Too bad! My mother had promised that, if I learned how to handle the fork and the knife, and how to eat without leaning my elbows on the table, she would invite King Mihai for dinner. Now I didn't have to try to eat nicely because we didn't have a king anymore. A priest used to come teach religion at my school. He was harsh, and we were afraid of him—and of God, too. But now we were taught there was no God, and the priest stopped coming of course. So we could be naughty and disobedient, since there was no God who could see us.

Maybe that was all I was able to understand about communism at that age. But I soon had chances to find out more.

Just like the dragon in a fairytale, the Communist Party "swallowed" and "destroyed" everything in its way. But where was our Prince Charming to slay him?

Everything people had earned up until then, after a lifetime of hard, honest work, was swallowed by that dragon in the name of the Party. People were stripped of their lands, houses, lives, freedom, conscience, joy and peace. Nobody owned anything anymore. The only owner was the State, the fierce dragon embodied by the Communist Party.

Everything was said to belong to the people, but who were the people? The people owned nothing, because the people themselves were owned by the State. Every citizen would work wherever the State sent him, would eat what the State would provide (which was almost nothing), and only after long ours of waiting in endless lines in front of the stores.

People standing in line to buy bread and groceries

My grandpa from Galați lost everything. However, he was "granted permission" to rent a room in one of the houses he had previously owned. My father's restaurant was closed up. Now there were six of us without any income. My grandfather from my mother's side was barely able to get a job, and happily it provided an income that allowed us to survive. At least we were still alive. There were many others who had lost their lives. People got arrested all around us. Many simply disappeared overnight. Terror was reigning in the country. The lines in front of the grocery shops seemed to have no end.

Mysterious Encounter

During that period ruled by terror I had a peculiar experience. One chilly spring morning my grandmother sent me to buy some eggs. It was right before Easter. She gave me a 100 lei bill—all the money she had left—and told me, "Take good care of it. Come back with the eggs and the change. Off you go!" I held the bill tight in my hand, and like any other child, I headed to the store, bouncing all the way.

I had quite a long distance to go—about fifteen minutes of walking. There was not a soul in the street so I kept hopping along merrily. About half way there I stopped to check if my treasure was still in place. I panicked, realizing my hand was empty. My knees started trembling. I headed back, trying to find the bill. Nothing. I returned again. Still nothing, as if the wind had taken that bill with it. I started crying my heart out. I could not go back home without the money.

All of a sudden a man appeared in front of me and asked, "Why are you crying, little girl?"

Terrified, I told him that I had lost my grandmother's money and I could not return home without it. He said to me with a gentle voice, "Don't cry anymore. Are you a Christian?"

"Yes," I replied. (We used to go to church every Easter.)

"Here you are, 100 lei. Pray for me when you go to church."

I felt embarrassed but I took the money, ran back home to grandma, handed the bill to her, and didn't go to buy anything anymore.

Who was that man? Who had made our paths cross? He was the first person who ever told me to pray, and back then I knew nothing about prayer!

My Cultural Religion

My parents and grandparents were Greek Orthodox Christians, which meant we used to go to church twice a year: on Easter and on Christmas. For me, Easter was all about eggs painted in red, while Christmas was about Santa.

Every Easter we went to church late in the evening, and at midnight we would light up the candles and sing, "Christ has risen, defeating death

. . ." The priest would say to the congregation, "Christ has risen," and we would answer, "He has risen indeed." Then we would return home with the candles in our hands lighting the night. It was a beautiful, impressive tradition. But the light of those candles was the only light we had about our Lord Jesus, His death and His resurrection.

As a child, Easter meant for me only red eggs and cake. We were able to bake cakes only if we could find eggs and sugar in the stores. Sometimes I would get something "new" to wear when mom would take some of the clothes that were too small for my brother and make them fit me.

New Life Under the Communist Regime

Life had changed completely. We now had new songs that praised the Communist Party, new shows that pictured the magnificent communist heroes, new newspapers that wrote about the party again, printing every day the photo of the president in their pages.

People were trying to grin and bear it by making fun of their misery, with the risk of losing their freedom. They would allude to the political situation, using jokes about "Bulă", a dumb student. One of those jokes went like this:

One day Bulă went to school with a wrinkled uniform. The teacher asked, "Why is your uniform wrinkled, Bulă?"

"Comrade, when my mom came back from work last night she was tired and she sat down to rest for a while. She plugged in the radio and heard the Comrade (the President) speaking. She turned it off. She plugged in the TV and heard the Comrade again. She turned the TV off, and after that she was afraid to plug the iron in, too."

I took life the way it was. I could not remember the time when we had had a free, beautiful, prosperous country. But my parents did, and they used to talk often about the good old days. The six of us lived in two rooms that served as kitchen as well. I was sharing one room with my parents, while Valentin shared the other one with my mom's parents.

Without running water, we had to go fetch it with the bucket from a pump in the inner court. We took turns washing ourselves in a wash bowl—in cold water, whether summer or winter. Only once a week did we get a warm bath with water heated on our cooking stove. The toilet was outside.

Holidays in Galați

Maybe the reason I loved holidays so much was that my parents used to send me by train to visit Grandpa Dimache and Grandma in Galați. Once I arrived in town, I took the tram and got off at the station that still bore Grandpa Dimache's name. When I finally met him, he used to kiss my cheeks and scratch me with his moustache. This is one of the special memories I have about those times . . .

Grandma

My grandmother had a more distant disposition, but she was a hardworking housewife. When I visited them for the winter holidays, my grandparents used to sleep in the kitchen, a warm room where they had one bed. I slept in the bedroom with Auntie Tinca, Grannie's sister. In order to save firewood, they lit the fire only before we went to sleep. The room was very cold, but the bed soft and comfortable. I would snuggle in close to Auntie Tinca, so after a while we would both get warm.

The summer holiday was even better. I would play outside all day long, and for lunch we had fish caught by Uncle Carol from the Danube River. Grandma used to cook lots of hominy and we would eat sitting around a table in the shade of a huge tree. The fish was full of tiny bones, but it was delicious. We were surrounded by lots of cats that would catch the leftovers we threw to them before they landed on the ground. Those memories made me fond of cats—and fish with hominy.

Teenage Years

When I was about 13, both my parents had a job. The state was the only master we knew. It would decide who was going to have a job, where that job would be and how much the employee would be paid. Nobody owned anything. The state had taken ownership of all the land, the buildings and the institutions. Since there were no more private owners to run the businesses and make sure the economic activities in the countryside or the cities were going well, the national economy was slowly ruined. Merchandise in the stores became scarce and food even scarcer. There was only a certain amount of food we were allowed to buy, according to a ration book we were given.

There was a period when we needed a certain number of points to buy clothing. Every person was given a number of points a month that could be used to buy clothes. For example if the price of a coat equalled 100 points, but the buyer had only 60 points, he or she had to wait until next month to get the monthly points and be able to buy that item.

The transportation systems, the banks, the media, and the schools were all owned by the state. The borders were closed and nobody was allowed to leave the "communist paradise". We were protected this way against the "capitalist danger".

The education system was changed as well. The seven gymnasium grades were compulsory and after that the students had two options. Those whose parents belonged to the lower, poor class, and had a "healthy origin" could go to high school, while those whose families had been wealthy in the previous regime could only go to a trade school and learn to master a vocation. Those who graduated from high school were prepared to continue their studies and go to the university.

As for me the access to high school was denied, so I ended up choosing the Chemistry Technical School.

Valentin's Miraculous Healing

Things got better at home. My parents were working, my grandparents moved in with Auntie Jenica, my mother's sister, and my brother Valentin moved into a doctor's garret. He had been accepted at the University and was studying History. He used his scholarship to pay his rent, so that left him with almost no money for food and heat in winter. He was hungry all the time.

My school was close to where he lived, but I was not allowed to go visit him all by myself. The winter of my first year in the technical school was terribly frosty. My brother sent word for me to come, because he was very sick. I decided to go see him even if I had to go alone. He was my brother after all, though only my half-brother.

That evening, after working in the lab, I headed toward his place. Climbing the steep and narrow stairs that led up to his garret I found him lying down with fever, coughing badly, and with no fire burning in the stove. He had no money for food or medicine. His eyes gleaming feverishly, he gave me a grateful smile.

I felt so sorry for him. He was my brother and I loved him so much. I had just received my own scholarship money—400 lei—that I used to help my parents with. Now I had to help my brother too, so I gave him 100 lei, telling myself I would make up an excuse to cover the missing money.

After a short visit I went down the stairs and walked to the tram station. The tram arrived soon. I got in and found an empty seat right in front of the door. Every time the tram stopped at a station, a chilly gust of air would blast through the doors. Thinking of my brother, I wondered what I was going to tell my parents about the missing money. I took the bills out of my pocket and started counting them in my lap. An empty seat on the other side of the tram was protected from the cold wind. Just as a passenger got up, ready to get off at the next stop, I gathered the bills from my lap and stood up.

As I was about to move to the empty seat I took a step and saw one 100 bill on the floor. I thought, "This would have been the last straw . . .

losing even the little money I was left with." I picked up the bill and sat down. Staring at the money again and counting, I could not believe my eyes. I had 400 lei! Not even 1 leu was missing. That meant that the bill on the floor was not mine. I could not understand how it had got there, because nobody had got on the tram or passed by, otherwise I would have noticed. Who had placed right there, in front of me, the exact amount I had given away? Back then I didn't realize I was witnessing a miracle, but now I know it without a doubt in my mind. (It was the second visible miracle in my life, and both involved the same amount of money.)

The plane was flying above the clouds. Putting an end to my daydreaming, burdensome questions were crossing my mind. "Where will the future take us?" "How are we going to live this wonderful and precious gift we call life?"

The plane was taking us to an airport, and then what? I told myself I would think about that later. The future would reveal itself to us.

We were all absorbed in our own thoughts. Vasile was very sad, and I didn't want to bother him with any questions. I felt overwhelmed as well, so I understood what he must have gone through. My thoughts returned to the past. I had never thought the cords of love could be so strong . . . they were pulling me back to all the things that had happened so far in our lives, none of which had been accidental. Every little detail had been orchestrated by the One who had created us and whom I had never known in my youth in spite of all the experiences I had been through.

The course of my life kept unfolding on the screen of my mind and my heart . . .

~ PART TWO ~
# All Grown Up

The Turmoil of My Soul

Somehow I was living what I used to call a "normal" life, not noticing the everyday inconveniences because I had grown used to them. However, an unexplainable sadness was robbing my life of joy and sucking the color out of everything.

I was at the age when people begin to ask themselves philosophical questions like "What kind of beings are we?" "Do we work only to secure our food and do we eat only in order to be able to work some more?" "Where is the joy in all that?" "What is the meaning of life?"

The communist schools were teaching evolution, declaring that human beings were nothing but matter, and that death put an end to everything. If that was true, what was the point of life? What were we going to live for if there was nothing after death, and if both those who lived fearing God and those who lived a wretched life would share the same fate? Why did we have feelings, ideals, desires, love, and appreciation for what was beautiful and good? Why were people able to sacrifice themselves for others, and why did they praise heroic acts? Why were there any heroes at all? How come everything in this world has a precise order, a meaning, a cause and a purpose? How come they don't just happen but follow certain laws, led by a high and perfect mathematics while we human beings—the most extraordinary creation—have accidentally appeared on this earth and are like leaves carried away by the wind? I was learning in school about the human body, and its complexity never ceased to amaze me. We are such wonderful beings! There's a perfect universe in every atom. Could that be a mere coincidence? What is energy? Where does matter, which communism had turned into an absolute, come from? What is the purpose of our existence in this world?

I had no answers for these questions, and sadness and discouragement were shrouding my heart. In order to ease my inner turmoil and sort out the typical teenage philosophical ideas in my head, I resorted to reading. I read a lot, so intensely relating to the stories in the books that I forgot about my own situation. I could imagine turning into different heroes or heroines who lived a happy or sad life in a world so wide that no one could set its boundaries. It was an artificial world . . . a world of dreams.

I decided I would become a theater producer. Valentin took me often to the theater or to concerts, and thus I began to love drama and classical music. But beyond this world of art, reality was really tough. Life in a communist country was as tightly closed as an oyster. We seemed to have a huge wall in front of us that blocked out everything else, a wall the symbol of communism was hanging on. But what was beyond that wall? We were not allowed to ask such questions. The system we lived in was limiting our horizon and we seemed to have no perspective at all.

Dad's Search for God

In the meantime my father had his own period of turmoil. His dad, Grandpa Dimache, had got diabetes after all the hardships and sufferings he had to go through. Because he didn't treat this problem in time his condition had worsened. A wound on one of his legs was not healing, and the doctor had told him he would have to amputate his leg. Grandpa asked my father what to do. The responsibility of making a decision was lying now on my father's shoulders and Dad was afraid to lose his father because of that surgery.

He was having a difficult time, and in such moments people remember God and ask for His help. My father was not a religious man but his desperation made him look for a divine sign. He went from church to church hoping he would find God somewhere. Whenever he found a church he entered the building and prayed, day after day, seeking and waiting. For what? I don't think he knew very well.

One of those days, while he was walking on Colței Street, his eyes focused on a small sign on one of the houses: "The Apostolic Pentecostal Church." He knew what church meant but he didn't know the meaning of the other two words. The building looked like an ordinary house, not a regular church. The door was open and he saw a large room with lots of wooden benches full of people. A tall, sturdy man with piercing, gentle eyes was standing in the doorway. My father stopped, and the kindness on that man's face encouraged him to ask, "What does this sign mean? I've never heard of such a church before!"

The man answered, "Listen to me, sir. If you're looking for God you will find Him here."

"Yes, I'm looking for God," my father said.

"Then come on in and take a seat. You will find Him here!"

And so my father entered. He sat on a bench and started to listen. At the end of the service the speaker announced: "We are going to pray now for the sick. Those of you who need healing, come up here."

Many of the people went up front and got down on their knees. Dad thought about his own problems. For a long time he'd had an eczema condition that no doctor had been able to treat. My mom did the best she could to help him, because she was working in a hospital. The eczema had spread from his legs to his arms and back, and it had recently appeared on his forehead as well. It didn't look pleasant at all and it was very itchy. He would take a warm bath every night and use some lotions to ease the itching.

Dad was thinking of his eczema, but he was ashamed to go in front of all the others. He was a proud man and did not want to join all those women who had answered the preacher's call. He told himself it would be better to just stand next to his bench, waiting to see if the healing would take place. However, after a while he knelt. The people in front of him were already in the front of the room. He didn't know what to say, but as an act of worship he got on his knees. All of a sudden he was pushed forward with such force that he fell over the bench in front of him. He got mad. Who had dared to hit him? He turned to see who had done that, and got really scared when he realized there was no one behind him, only empty benches. It was enough to make his hair stand on end. He didn't know what to think of it. He returned home silent and thoughtful, saying not a word. Who would have believed such a story?

That evening my mom warmed the water for him as usual. When he took off his clothes to bathe himself he was shocked! His skin was as soft and healthy as a baby's. The eczema was completely gone. He could hear the words of the man in the church's doorpost echoing in his ears, "You will find God here!" Maybe that was the first time in my father's life he had really looked for God, and the truth was that God was the one who found him.

My father began attending that church regularly. After a while he started telling us about "salvation" and "the sacrifice of the Lord Jesus", but we couldn't understand what he was talking about. However, my mother and I noticed that Dad had changed a lot. He called this transformation "being born again". The change in his life was so obvious that my mom got upset and said to him, "What kind of man have you turned yourself into? Don't you like to have fun anymore? What kind of life are you offering your own child? All you do now is go to that poor church. What's the point of praying all the time?"

In a way I thought she was right. Dad was a different man now, and I could not understand how and where we had lost him. He was completely changed. Still, I felt so sorry for him! He never argued with my mom—he only listened to her, smiling kindly—but kept on following his Lord. He was suffering silently. Sometimes I could overhear him praying for my mother. For his sake I started going with him to church. The believers called it "assembly" because it was a simple gathering of people. There were no stained glass windows, no icons or candles like in the churches I was used to. Everything was different. The people were very friendly. They sang beautifully, and I loved it. Their life was so simple. It lacked any refinement, any pretention, any display of superiority.

Nevertheless, I had never met more content people. I figured they were not like all the others because they were not very educated. But soon I realized there were doctors and engineers among them, who acted just like the other believers and didn't brag about their diplomas. What and who gave them such inner peace and joy? Where was that glint and confidence in their eyes coming from?

I felt comfortable in their midst. They accepted me, though I was not one of them. They spoke often about the "receiving of the faith" but I did not quite understand what there was to be received. Perhaps they meant unbelievers had to receive Jesus as Lord. But how could He be received? And why? However, it was obvious they had received something. And that something was extremely desirable.

After a while my mother decided she had had enough of that kind of living and gave Dad one last warning: "You either give up your faith, or we break up."

Their talk about divorce made my blood run cold. I could already picture myself having to choose between staying with one and leaving the other, and the idea was unthinkable.

But Dad said to Mom, "I don't want us to get a divorce. We've been together for a lifetime. I will never leave you, but you must understand that I will never leave my faith either."

He was determined to stick with his faith and follow through with his newfound path. Their arguments did not end there, but it was obvious that Dad had become a new person. Before coming to Christ, he had been a big smoker. If he felt like smoking in the middle of the night and he ran out of cigarettes, he would get out of bed and start roaming the streets until he met someone willing to give him one. He couldn't live without his cigarettes. He was never able to break free of this addiction until he became a believer.

After quite a long time and lots of polemics, my mom started to accept the situation. My dad was a changed man, but he had changed for the better. He was no longer the selfish man who expected to be served and did whatever he wanted. He was ready now to help anyone with his words or actions, and he started to care about those around him. It would be difficult to leave a good man after spending a lifetime at his side. True, he didn't accompany us anymore to all kinds of shows and performances, but he did not stop us from going. I am sure he prayed for us once we left the house. Maybe that's why we didn't enjoy going there without him.

My First Bible

On one of the Sundays I went to church with my dad, somebody there gave me a Bible. It was an extraordinary gift, because no Bibles were printed or sold in Romania under the communist regime. Such activities were forbidden back then. The communists had declared there was no God, and the Bible was considered a fairytale book. However I could not stop wondering why it had been forbidden if all it contained was fairytales. The other fairytale books had not shared the same fate and could be bought in any bookstore. So I concluded the Bible must have been valuable, since the communists hated it so much. I had already found out that the Bible was the holy book given to mankind by God; I started reading it and discovered it to be very enjoyable. Books had always been my refuge, but the Bible was different from all the others. I started reading it from its beginning, the way any book is supposed to be read, and after a while I realized that nothing happened accidentally. I understood that we were created by God and we belonged to our Creator. It was as if I had found a purpose in life, a balance, as if I had discovered I was valuable. The things I found in the Bible were like a buried treasure. I kept reading eagerly, but after a while I got stuck and could not follow the subject anymore. Then I skipped to the end like any reader does when he or she can't wait to see how a books ends. There, on the last pages of the Bible, I encountered God, His Son and all those who believed in Him reigning on the throne. The Bible was indeed a wonderful book with such a beautiful ending.

My mind understood it and I liked what I was reading, but the message had not penetrated my heart yet. The chapters in the Bible that described Creation illuminated my mind, helping me understand many of the laws governing nature that I had learned about in school. Now they were finally making sense.

The church on Colței Street that I used to go to with my dad did not emphasize the topic of Creation. It seldom even taught about God the Father. Listening to the messages there I understood that God was perfection itself, and everything that did not share the same perfection would perish one day. If a bright light begins to shine in a pitch black room, the darkness can no longer be dark. It will be absorbed by the light. Likewise we, as imperfect beings, had no chance to stand in the presence of God. However, He was the One who created us and could grant us access to Him through His Son. The sermons in church focused more on the person of Jesus Christ, the Son of God. While listening to those who explained the Bible, the divine light was slowly penetrating my heart. I understood that the Bible was not so much a science or history book, but God's love message for all mankind.

Oh, how I longed for that love! God created man to be His own child and gave him everything. He created for him animals and fishes, birds, flowers and fruits, the starry sky, but more than anything God loved man and wanted to have fellowship with him. However, man—God's perfect creation that could be fulfilled only in the presence of the Father—allowed the evil one to deceive him into believing that he could have even more without God. It was as if one tooth would jump out of the mouth and would try to become someone leaving the whole body aside; or as if an eye would leave the body, attempting to create a world of its own. But this is not possible. When you are created by a divine mind it's best for you to stay where you were meant to be. That's the only way we can enjoy God's blessings. We are not gods to create a new order; we must take the place the Creator has assigned to us. We have only one life to live, so it's not worth trying to experiment outside God's will. He is the Creator and He made us. We are not His equals. We did not create anything good in this world. We only used His creation, but we did not create anything. It is crystal clear.

In physics classes we learned that our planet was given a certain quantity of energy. We are not able to create more or to destroy it, but we can transform and use it. Who gave earth this energy? The life we have was given to us; we did not give it to ourselves, we can't create it or put an end to it. We can use it for a good purpose or we can choose to waste it. Creation belongs to God and is governed by His rules. If we respect them they will work for our best, but if we break them we'll suffer the consequences.

I understood in that period that God was just. But how does His justice coexist with His love? How could we expect a perfect God—in whose presence nothing imperfect can stand—to grant us His mercy? No matter how hard we would try to earn His favor we wouldn't stand a chance. However, true life can be found only in His presence. When I realized that, I began to pay more attention to the message about Jesus Christ that was being preached in church.

Secret Home Groups

We used to meet secretly in small groups in the believers' houses for fear the Secret Police agents might discover us. They were always lurking around, looking for such activities, and that's why we had to stay low.

The official gathering in the church building that took place twice a week was controlled by the authorities, who allowed only those who had their approval to speak to the congregation. This is why we had other secret meetings in the houses.

After a while my father got Mom's approval to have such "assemblies" in our home as well. I was very glad. I used to clean the house, bake some cookies, and eagerly await our brothers and sisters. They arrived silently, one by one or in groups of two or three, trying not to make themselves noticed. They kept coming until our house was full. They seemed so beautiful to me with their kind faces, bright eyes and warm speech. Their conduct was humble and grateful, but fearless nevertheless, because they trusted God's unseen protection.

There were about fifteen or twenty of us crowded into one room and we had to move the furniture around to fit all of us. Our guests would sit on chairs, on the bed or even on the floor.

Our meetings would always start with prayer. The believers prayed in unison and didn't mind that they could hear one another. They used to pray for us every time, asking God to open our hearts to receive the Lord. One wondered how it was possible to open one's heart...

A warm feeling touched my heart during their prayer, and tears would fill my eyes. I would not have changed that feeling for anything in the world.

We kept the windows closed for fear the neighbors might hear us and report to the Secret Police, but that never happened. After the prayer, the believers started to sing. Oh, how beautiful those moments were! They knew most of the songs by heart and others were written by hand in notebooks they brought with them. Most of the songs were hymns that praised God. How sweet their words were compared to the ones we had to sing for the Communist Party! We were all sick and tired of the glory the Party attributed to itself. But in those meetings we did what was right and we gave all the praise to God.

After singing a few songs we would all wait for somebody to open the Bible, read a passage and explain it to us. That was when we opened the windows to get some fresh air.

I would listen intently to the message, trying to understand what I heard. This way, evening after evening, in our house or at others where Dad would take me, I had the chance to learn more about the love of God.

Of course I knew about the Trinity—God the Father, God the Son and God the Holy Spirit. I had heard about it in the Orthodox Church when we used to bow down and make the sign of the cross. We would put three fingers together and touch them to our forehead while saying, "In the Name of the Father...", continuing to our right shoulder and the words, "In the Name of the Son...", and finishing with the left shoulder saying, "In the Name of the Holy Spirit." So this was what I knew about the Trinity. But how little that was! It was time for me to learn more about the Son, and later on about the Holy Spirit.

After the Biblical passage was explained and the fellowship ended, it was my turn to serve the guests with sweets while we talked. Each believer wanted to know how the others were doing, if they had faced particular needs and if they needed help. Sometimes they would take an offering for a family in need. I was amazed by all this. None of our relatives or friends would have cared if we were in trouble. But though these people were not related by blood they called each other brothers and sisters, and they acted like ones.

Their love helped me feel the love of God the Son. Yes, God the Father is just; the wages of sin is death, and eternal separation from the Father. I had no chance to be in His presence. But the Father gave His only Son to pay the price and redeem me through His death. He didn't have to pay for His own sin because He was perfect, just like the Father. Jesus gave His own life for mine. He is the only way we can get to the Father. Thanks to Him, the guilt of my sin is not terrifying me anymore. My debt was paid by Him. This is how the law of justice could be satisfied and we were set free, without the heavy punishment hanging heavy above our heads. This is why we can lift our eyes to heaven, full of humility and gratitude. Our Lord Jesus did all this for me, and for all mankind. We find this truth written in the Bible: "For God so loved the world that He gave His only begotten Son that whosoever believes in Him should not perish but have everlasting life" (John 3:16).

My Lord Jesus had become very dear to my soul. He had been so patient with me.

My First Job

I had graduated from the Chemistry Technical School but I still wanted to become a theater producer. In order to begin my studies in this field I needed a diploma in Philology first. The entrance examination for that faculty was really difficult, and the school I had graduated from did not prepare me for that exam. I tried, though it was like banging my head against a brick wall, and of course I failed.

Then I got a job—my first job. I was a laboratory technician at the lab of Emilia Irza Pediatric Hospital in Bucharest. I didn't like it, and I couldn't take my mind off the theater. But at least I was able to help my parents with my income.

In the meantime my brother Valentin had married a physical training teacher from the faculty where he had studied history. He moved into her apartment. Actually they used only one room in a three room apartment and shared the bathroom, kitchen and living room with other two families. I enjoyed visiting him. Their apartment house had a heating system (so he didn't have to use firewood anymore). They had warm water in the kitchen and the bathroom (he no longer had to bring water from the pump in the backyard). But best of all was the fact that the toilet seat was in the bathroom, not outside.

I soon became very good friends with my sister-in-law. She was a lively, cheerful, friendly young woman. After she got married she had the same name as I did, Elena Radu. I was Miss Elena Radu and she was Mrs. Elena Radu.

I was still very fond of my brother, whom I loved perhaps even more than I would have if we'd shared both our parents. He was a really special young man. He didn't laugh a lot but he made us burst our sides with laughter. I admired him because he was able to explain everything, especially history, so clearly and captivating that we didn't even notice how fast time flew. Now he was teaching history at a high school. He was loved by his students, and the girls liked him for his attractive appearance.

Valentin

In summer I used to ride my bike to work because it was quite far, and I didn't want to pay for all three means of transportation needed to get there.

On the way to work I had plenty of time to think and make plans for the future. I was wondering if I would find someone to marry, if my

The tram

future husband and I would be able to live in an apartment with running water and a toilet in our bathroom, and if we would have a car and the chance to travel and see the world.

Of course all these were mere fantasies, the kind of dreams a girls has about meeting her own Prince Charming and moving into a fairytale castle. With such dreams in my mind I arrived at work where I had to face reality again: blood tests, sick and scared children that cried a lot. Their suffering made me sad. Their parents were not allowed to come in with them. The rooms were overcrowded and the little ones were afraid when they saw the medical staff dressed in white overalls, knowing that needles were waiting for them.

The Chemistry Faculty

A year passed by, then one beautiful spring day, when everybody was enjoying the renewal of nature and hoping the new season would bring with it a good change, I heard about the opportunity of a new job as a laboratory technician at the Chemistry Faculty.

There I was introduced to Mrs. Pirtea, the lab head. She liked me and agreed to hire me. My job was to prepare the labs for the university students. The Chemistry Technical School and the hospital experience proved to be helpful. I had all the knowledge needed for that position. My new job was easier, more enjoyable, cleaner and closer to home. Mrs. Pirtea got to like me soon.

Once spring was over the school year ended, the students' vacation started, and there was not much for me to do anymore.

One day Mrs. Pirtea told me, "Listen to me, girl! Prepare for the admittance exam in the fall. I give you permission to come to work every day and study here. You have all summer long to get ready and you can apply for the entrance exam at the Chemistry Faculty. You have all the books you need here, and I will help you all I can. Forget about your theater dreams (I had told her about my plans of becoming a theater producer). Theater will not make you a living, but chemistry will."

I went home and told my parents about her advice, and they were excited. I told myself I could try the theater business later. So I set aside my dreams about the theater world and willy-nilly I began to study. Mrs. Pirtea was watching my progress and I didn't want to disappoint her. I wanted to succeed for her sake, but I didn't really like what I was studying. The science of Chemistry was too exact for my taste and it didn't match my desire to live in a world of fantasy and imagination where I could be a queen one day and a servant the next. I could die in one act and come back to life in the following one. Actors could laugh or cry, but those feelings did not get inside them because they were just playing a role. Their inner lives were empty, and they were too sad to face reality and their real selves. That was a truth I came to understand only later.

I spent that summer studying. The whole building was silent and empty because the students had gone home for summer vacation. The massive building protected me against the heat that was gripping the entire city and Mrs. Pirtea was my guardian angel with whom I had found favor.

When summer ended and the examination period neared I felt lost. The competition was tough and I was afraid I was not going to make it.

I was not very excited to study chemistry, but I didn't want to disappoint Mrs. Pirtea.

To everybody's delight (mine included) I passed the exam, and at nineteen I started my first year as a student at the Chemistry Faculty of the Bucharest University. It sounded terrific. My enthusiasm was contagious, but once the classes started, my excitement faded, as I had to study more and more.

Life as a university student had its pleasant and unpleasant sides. It was completely different from high school. The students felt like they were enjoying complete freedom. They didn't have to attend the classes. The professors would teach and explain the topics we were supposed to cover, but nobody asked us if we were studying anything at all. Therefore we typically postponed it, thinking we had plenty of time. But the exam period was getting closer, and only later we realized we should have used that "free" time during the school semester and dedicate it to studying. We would have to work hard every day if we wanted to pass our finals and get our diploma.

The experience of those years helped me understand the meaning of our life here, on earth. We are all enrolled in the school of life, and we think that everything—parents, education, love—revolves around us. We tend to believe that the time we are given, the time of our life, can be taken for granted and that we can use it according to our heart's desire. We make no effort to understand the meaning of life and we never think that the teaching we received in the first grades of life is not accidental, but has a higher purpose we don't even pay attention to. We don't think we'll have to face our finals when the great Professor who has allowed us to prepare for one whole semester, or year or a lifetime will no longer be our teacher but our examiner and will ask us what we've achieved during the time period we were given. When we stand in front of Him for the final exam of our life, we will get a diploma that will grant us access to heaven, or we will painfully fail for eternity. And we will not be given the chance to repeat this last exam.

This thought should make us shudder, especially if we are in the habit of wasting our time.

In those years I used to go to school during the weekdays, and on Sundays I liked going to the church on Calea Moșilor, pastored by Brother Pantelimon Cojocaru. The church on Colței Street had been closed by the communist authorities.

Now I was going to church because I liked it, not only to please my dad. I felt good in the house of the Lord and my heart was filled there with peace and joy. The gathering of the believers was refreshing my soul; it was my source of energy.

On Sundays I often used to go to both the morning and evening services. The mornings were usually consecrated to Bible study, which I liked, while the evenings hosted joyful youth programs that warmed my heart. Many times I went to church on Thursdays too, because that was the weekday when believers were allowed to get together in the church building. I would get there quite late, after the evening classes or after work. In summer I would listen to the sermon from outside, looking through the open windows. I was not the only one outside, since the building was full. The air was not as hot out there, but I had to stand by the window.

Born Again

One Sunday morning my father and I took the tram to church. I was trying to read the posters I saw outside. Most of them were advertising movies or theater plays (which were my favorite). I wanted to pick up one for that afternoon.

I will never forget that day. We got to church and we sat on a bench as usual. I was only a spectator. I don't remember who preached that day or what the sermon was about; all I know is that when the pastor asked if there was anyone who wanted to receive the Lord as his or her personal Savior, to be forgiven and to become a child of God, something wonderful happened to me. Words cannot describe what I felt that moment. My heart was flooded by gentle warmth, deep love, honest gratefulness and humble courage. An unseen hand strengthened my shaking knees, enabling me to stand in front of all the others and accept that heavenly invitation.

What happened in that moment? What kind of chemical or spiritual metamorphosis took place inside of me? How were all my priorities and desires rearranged? Who could know or understand it? How can a person be changed in the twinkling of an eye in such a radical and heavenly way?

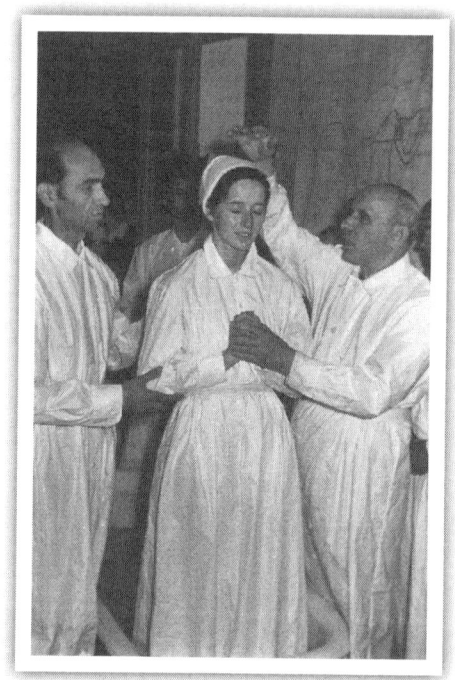

I felt as if I was floating in the clouds; I was happy, and tears of joy were streaming down my face while I was hugging all those who came to welcome me into the spiritual family of their Lord, who had just become my Lord as well. He was no longer only Lord and Savior; now he was my Lord and Savior. I could feel His presence, His smiling face and open arms. I felt as if I had been born again.

The prayer I whispered that moment, and many other times in my life, went like this: "Lord, don't You ever leave me or allow me go my own ways, because they will never lead to anything good. Keep me in You, in Your arms, in Your will, by Your power and for Your glory!"

Brother Caraman and Brother Cojocaru at my baptism ceremony

A few months later I was baptized by Brother Caraman and Brother Cojocaru. It was the 24th of September, 1958.

Mom Receives the Faith

To my father's delight, Mom started coming to church with us. At first she came all dressed up, with lots of jewelry, and in the midst of those modest people she looked like a peacock. But the Spirit of the Lord is not looking at the outside like people do. He is looking at the heart, and we lived to see the day when God's Spirit penetrated her heart, too.

What wonderful grace and blessing it was to have our sins forgiven, to belong to a family whose father was the heavenly One and whose older brother was Jesus Himself, the One who showed us His love by sacrificing His own life for our sake. It was our turn now to love Him and to prove our love and gratefulness by living in obedience.

Everything seemed to be perfect now. Our family was united by faith, love and the desire to live together according to the teachings of God's Holy Word. But we were only at the beginning of our walk with the Lord. There was so much more to learn.

My father was now preaching in church. He had a special exhortation gift. He often went to different prayer groups that gathered in houses. He visited the sick and the needy, and he always had a word of encouragement for every believer.

I went on with my studies. The activities my fellow students were involved in did not attract me anymore. The theater and the stage no longer interested me. Now I had the truth and I didn't need the lie anymore. I cautiously tried to witness the Lord to those around me, but I could see they were afraid to listen to me because they could have got in trouble if the communist authorities found out. It was easy to be kicked out of school for ideological reasons, and the Communist Party did not encourage faith in God.

~ PART THREE ~

Learning Endurance
The Storm Is Coming

We were experiencing the calm before the storm. Our family was enjoying a time of serenity and joy, songs and thankfulness. Both my parents had jobs, and I was a university student. But the storm was coming and the testing of our faith was right at our door.

We were living in a communist country. The atheist beast was given absolute power, and it did not allow the people to worship or serve anyone else. Those who knew the true God were standing in its way and had to be removed. That's the fate that would have waited for us if God weren't on our side. He is a living and true God who doesn't promise to deliver us from every trouble, just that He will hold us in His arms while going through it with us.

We did not know much about persecution. Why would we be persecuted? We had learned to live like good citizens, to love our neighbors, to make an honest living, to help each other, to tell the truth for the sake of the One who gave His life for us. It was easy for us to be Christians when all was going well. But the Lord Himself had to suffer, though He lived a perfect life.

Dad Is Arrested

The storm started with my father's arrest. His zeal for exhorting the other believers and for preaching the Word had not gone unnoticed by the Secret Police. He had to be silenced, so they planned a setup at work and charged him for not reporting that a fellow worker had stolen some items. Though there was no evidence to prove his guilt, my father was sentenced to six years of prison. The news struck us like a bolt out of the blue—six years of prison and the seizing of all our belongings.

A car pulled over in front of our house, several men entered, and took almost everything we had. We were left with one bed, a table, two chairs, two plates and two sets of flatware. We were not rich, but we had had all the necessities. The truth was that the robbery did not even bother us. My mother and I were so grieved by dad's arrest that nothing else mattered. Tears were streaming down our faces but that did not impress anybody. Those men were used to such emotions. If they didn't do their job they would have ended up just like us.

We wondered, "God, do You see what is going on here?"

The Lord saw it all, and He was just as grieved as we were. Suffering cleanses and reveals the depths of the human heart. We expected to be avoided now by our new friends for fear of the persecution. But they did not stay away from us. The news about our trouble spread like wildfire in our group. The unity of God's family was demonstrated right away. We did not call one another brothers and sisters for no reason. They came one after another to encourage and help us. Two beloved brothers who

Brother Constantin Caraman   Brother Costache Ioanid

were as close to us as my own parents, Brother Caraman and Brother Ioanid, carried a wardrobe on their shoulders for quite a long distance so that we would have a place to keep our clothes. The distance alone would have wearied for their weak bodies, even without carrying that piece of furniture.

They said to us, "It's not much, but at least you will be able to keep your things inside."

We could hear the Lord telling us through them, "Do not be afraid. I am with you and I will watch over you and your father as well."

My daily routine included visits to the lawyer, the courthouse, the university, the house groups and the Sunday gathering. I could no longer focus on my studies. During that stormy period I was able to find peace for my soul in the house prayer meetings. My favorite place to go was to the Man family's home.

One such prayer meeting lasted until dawn, and after that I went straight to school. My heavy head was almost falling on my notebook and I could barely keep my eyes open but I tried not to attract attention. At some point I noticed a few fleas jumping on the white pages of my notebook. I almost burst into laughter and I felt wide awake. Once I got home I dealt with those impertinent parasites.

It's not easy to explain what was going on in our life. Knowing we could do nothing to help Dad was painful, but we knew we were not alone or deserted in all this. We felt God's presence beside us.

We did not have any other income besides my mom's salary and that was not enough to cover both our expenses and the cost of the food parcel we sent periodically to Dad. I decided to drop out of school and get a job, but the other believers advised me not to give up but to stay there for as long as the authorities would allow me to. I listened to them, though I found it very difficult.

My father had been taken to a labor camp in the Bărăgan Plain, with thousands of other prisoners. The labor camp was in a place called Balta Albă (The White Pond). I had no idea where it got that name from because the pond on the map was only a black spot. In order to get there I had to take the train from Bucharest to Dorobanți, and then walk for a few more kilometers.

We were allowed to visit Dad once a month, and then we could bring him a food parcel too. The trip was long and most of the time I went to see him all by myself. My mom could not take a day off work to join me when the visits were scheduled. I was almost 21 back then and that tough life made me stronger. I didn't pay attention to my weariness or physical weakness. I didn't care about the obstacles because the Lord was my strength. I called upon His Name to protect me and help me find favor in the eyes of men. And yet the moments spent in the company of other visitors in a tiny, dirty room full of flies, waiting for the inmates to return from work, were heartbreaking. We could see them coming when they were still far away. They were exhausted. When they got closer to the waiting room they lifted their heads and looked around, hoping they would see a familiar face. We had a chance to talk for a little while, though my dad was behind bars, and we both started pretending. I told him we were hoping he would be set free soon and that my mom and I were doing fine, while he pretended to believe me and tried to convince me he was OK too. But we both knew that God was our only hope. The few minutes we were allowed to spend together passed quickly so we looked at each other for one last time, trying to smile, but could not hide the deep sadness and the tears in our eyes. Then I would turn and cry all the way back home. That part of the trip seemed the most difficult of all, though I had no food parcel to carry anymore.

Brother Richard and Sister Binția

One Thursday evening, after my hours of practice in the lab were over, I went to church. There was still time to listen to a few minutes of the sermon before the end of the meeting and to see my brothers and sisters.

It was a warm evening so the windows were open. Some believers were standing outside by the windows and I joined them. I noticed a tall, middle-aged gentleman I had never seen before, and at the end of the service we started to talk. During that interesting conversation he told me he was a Jew and asked me if I wanted to learn Hebrew. I was so excited that it didn't take long for him to convince me to go meet his family, all the more so as he lived a few minutes away from our home.

That night marked the beginning of a new stage in my life as a believer; it was as if I had passed from kindergarten to the first grade in the school of faith. This is how I met the Wurmbrands, Richard, Sabina and their son Mihai.

Richard and Sabina Wurmbrand

Sister Binția

I didn't see Brother Richard many times after that because he was arrested again. But the relationship with his wife, Sister Binția as close friends used to call her, changed my life. I became her spiritual child—one of many—because there were lots of others who were strengthened by her teaching and her living example. I used to visit her almost daily. Many believers visited her evening after evening, eager to receive a Bible message, a teaching drawn from life, a piece of advice or a smile. She had no time for herself and her own pain. She had dedicated her life to comforting others.

Her place was a refuge for many believers hounded by the Communists' hatred, many precious people who were deeply humiliated by that hostile regime but deeply loved by God, regardless of their denomination.

That was where I discovered how many there were who had not given up their faith, in spite of the threats they faced and even the danger of losing their freedom. There certainly was a price to be paid but it was no match for the price God paid to set us free. He sacrificed the life of His only Son, Jesus Christ, who died a terrible death to redeem us from our sins. Yes, if I had to sacrifice something for the sake of my Lord, He was definitely worth it.

Memories with Sister Binția

I have many precious memories of my Sister Binția. When I came home from school in the evening I used to stop by her place on Olteni Street to spend a few moments with her. Some words from the Bible and a prayer were always waiting for me there. Believers would visit her every day for advice, prayer or exhortations from the Scripture. She was like a refreshing spring of water for all the thirsty souls. I never heard her complaining about anything or talking about the suffering she had to go through. Her entire life was dedicated to serving others.

One day a brother came to her and started complaining about another believer. Since I was too young to be part of the discussion I often stayed in a corner, waiting until Sister Binția had a little time for me too. After that brother left, Sister Binția looked at me with deep sadness in her eyes and said, "You see, dear Pușa, it's so easy to judge others and forget that no tree is slanting because it wants to. It must be going through a strong storm that makes it slant. The same happens to us humans. Nobody knows the storm the one who is judged is going through, and nobody knows what he or she would have done in the same situation. It's so easy to judge the people around us."

Another time, one afternoon when I was there, a sister came to her complaining about her son who had gone astray though he had been raised in church.

"I don't know what to do anymore," that sister said. "I scolded him, I told him how bad all the things he was doing were, I punished him—but all in vain. Now he's avoiding me while doing only what he wants. What can I do to change that?"

"Telling him how bad his behavior is does not help," said Sister Binția. "He already knows that, maybe even better than you do. It's no use telling him how he should behave either. He knows that very well, since he's been raised in the house of the Lord. All you need to do is to mirror God's love through your love for him in all the circumstances you face. Help him understand that you love him even when it hurts. Talk to him about our Lord Jesus. He's the only one who can help your son; never cease praying to Him because only the Spirit of the Lord has the key that can unlock the door of any heart. Rebukes and reproaches are not very helpful, especially at this age."

One winter night I went to bring Sister Binția some firewood I had managed to save from our own quota. I didn't have many pieces, so I was able to carry them in my arms, and I thought I would make her a nice surprise. In those days we got a certain quota of firewood and most of it was wet, so people would light a fire only when it was really necessary.

The snow was deep, but it was nice and quiet outside. When Sister Binția saw the firewood her face brightened up, and with a playful look in her eyes she went in the other room and returned with some firewood too.

"Dear Pușa, the Lord has sent you," she said. "I was hoping you would come. Look, I have some firewood too, that I have set aside. Let's go now to the Ciopraga family. They were granted permission to immigrate to Israel and this is the last night they will spend here. They handed all their belongings over to the state, and now they sleep on a blanket on the hard floor, in a freezing cold room. They have packed everything and they will go in the morning to the airport. Let's take the firewood to them so they will not freeze tonight. Come with me to carry the firewood there and wish them a blessed trip."

I had had a different plan in mind. I had thought about her and her needs, but her word was precious to me and I had learned to respect it.

"All right, Sister Binția, but I brought the firewood for you."

"Come on, don't worry about me. I have a comforter and a bed to keep me warm."

So not wasting any time, we left to visit the Ciopragas. Walking side by side through the deep, fresh layer of snow was pleasant for me, because I was young and tall so my long legs could move easily through the snow. But Sister Binția was a short woman. The snow reached up to her knees and she struggled through it. I gave her an affectionate look and found myself thinking out loud when I said, "How I wish I could carry you in my arms so that you don't have to struggle through this snow!"

She laughed and then added seriously, "Many times we wish we could carry the burdens of our loved ones, to make their life easier. But that can't be done. Each one of us has his own destiny and burdens that nobody can carry for him."

Later on I remembered those words so often!

I could write volumes about Sister Binția but I will stop here. For me, the most important thing is that she was a real spiritual mother in my life, and that's how I will always remember her.

Food Relief to Lătești

It was the summer of 1960, when the darkness of the communist regime and the dictatorship of the brutal Secret Police pervaded the whole country. One day Sister Binția told me the story of the Reformed Christian family of Pastor Francisc Viski. He had been sentenced to prison for many years. His wife and their seven small children had been evicted from their house in a village close to Oradea and were deported to Lătești, the so called "misery village" in the middle of Bărăgan Plain. How many tears have watered that dry land! My father was incarcerated in a labor camp situated in the same area.

One day my mom and I were informed about when we were scheduled to visit Dad. That meant I was going to see him soon and could bring him some clothes and food. Our income was barely enough to live from hand to mouth, but the love of several brothers and sisters in Christ turned into an indescribable generosity. This made us feel we were not alone and helpless.

I had to go visit my father all alone because mom could not take a day off. With a joyful heart I went to share the good news with Sister Binția. I felt as welcome in her garret as in my own house. I told her about the trip I was going to make and, as expected, she shared my joy. Just like us, she was lacking the love and protection of her husband who had been imprisoned too. I told her I was going to take the train from Bucharest to Dorobanți and then walk the several kilometers from the train station to Balta Albă.

Sister Binția remembered that Pastor Francisc Viski's family had been deported and was under house arrest in the village of Lătești, close to Fetești, a town I was going to pass through on my way to Dorobanți. The train was going to stop in Fetești for 10 or 15 minutes. Not far from there lived Iuliana Viski, a young mom, and her seven kids.

Sister Binția also told me about Marica, the "angel" who helped this family. Marica was a young lady who had helped Iuliana raise the children before they were deported. After that unhappy event, she was free to go wherever she wanted, but she gave up her freedom and followed Iuliana to that wretched village. She chose to stand by their side though she was free.

Sister Binția had a suggestion for me, "Would you like to carry some food for the Viski family and give it to Sister Marica? She will wait for you at the train station in Fetești. She's not under house arrest. You know, the train stops there a little longer than in other stations."

I accepted the wonderful plan gladly. On visiting day I took dad's parcel, and then I went to Sister Binția's for the food for the Viskis. When I got there I could not believe my eyes. The food I was supposed to take to Sister Iuliana filled eleven parcels of all sizes, and in their midst there was a heavy suitcase I couldn't even lift from the floor.

When she saw my puzzled look, Sister Binția said, "Don't get upset. We'll help you get to the train station; when you get close to Fetești all you have to do is drag the parcels to the door. The train will stop there for about ten minutes and Marica will wait for you there. She will take all the parcels to Lătești, to the Viski family."

Her plan sounded reasonable enough and I did as I was told. I got on the train but I kept on getting in and out of my compartment to check how much longer until the train arrived in Fetești. About half an hour early I dragged all the parcels to the door. Once the train came to a halt I started shouting, "Marica! Marica!"

In the bustling train station my shouts went unnoticed. I kept on calling "Marica" for ten minutes, until the train got going again, taking me and all those parcels further away.

Dumbfounded, I stood in the hallway staring at all that luggage. "Lord, what am I going to do?" I wondered, and started praying. I could have "forgotten" the parcels in the train, but seven hungry children were waiting for food and I could not take those parcels to them all by myself.

While I kept on wondering what to do, the train stopped in Dorobanți, my final destination. A soldier who "happened" to get off at the same station asked me, "Do you need some help, miss?"

And so, during the short minute the train was halted in that station all my parcels were placed on the platform. I managed to carry them close to a small booth, and the train dispatcher allowed me to leave them there until I returned with the evening train.

I took my dad's parcel and got going on the dusty road to Balta Albă, praying that God would make me a blessing for him during his difficult trial. Dad was an innocent man locked behind bars like a criminal and treated worse than an animal. When I arrived there I had to wait as usual for the prisoners to return from work. After a while I saw then dragging their exhausted feet through the dusty road in the heat of the summer day. Dad saw me and smiled sadly. Somebody had finally come to visit him.

Late that night I walked all the way back to the train station. I had forgotten for a while about the luggage complication, but now I had to face it again. The parcels were waiting for me where I had left them. Nothing was missing, even though nobody had kept an eye on them.

The several people who were returning from the prison as well helped me put all that luggage back on the train. I don't even remember how I carried that huge, heavy suitcase inside.

The darkness outside seemed to have settled in my heart as well. I remained in the hallway to be alone and pray. The hot air in the train was stuffy, so I leaned my forehead against the cool window, looking out into the dark. I didn't want to see or hear anyone while I began to pray, "Lord, what should I do? Somewhere in Lătești there are seven hungry children. But where is this village and how can I carry all these parcels there? It's dark already and I'm so tired. What is Your will, Lord?"

The empty hallway was just the spot for my unspoken prayers. At the right moment a woman emerged from one of the compartments. I thought she wanted to pass by, but she stopped next to me. I made room for her to pass but she didn't. She just stayed there as if she were my travel companion. I was watching her out of the corner of my eye, obviously bothered by her presence. How was I supposed to keep on praying? Though the appearance of the unknown woman was not unpleasant, I was not enjoying her company. She was standing too close to me, seeming eager to wade in.

A few moments later she started questioning me. "Are all these parcels yours?" She looked at the pile of luggage.

"Yes."

"Where are you going?"

"To Bucharest," I replied coldly.

I was not in a talking mood, but she didn't care and kept on asking, "Are you going right to Bucharest?"

I thought she might have been sent by the Secret Police to question me, but nobody had followed me there. I found myself answering, "I think I will stop in Fetești."

"Right in Fetești?"

"No, not quite." What an impossible woman! I said to myself, now really annoyed.

"But where exactly?"

"To Lătești," came my irritated answer.

"But who are you visiting there?"

"Lady, listen, I have my own troubles and I don't really feel like talking."

"That's OK, dear, we all have our own troubles. Just tell me who you are going to visit in Lătești," she persisted.

What an exasperating woman!

"A family with seven children," I said evasively, hoping she would leave me alone.

"And what is the name of that family? Oh, you must be talking about the pastor's wife! I bet it is her. I know her very well; she gives piano lessons!"

Trying once again to end the conversation I said, "I don't care who is giving who piano lessons, and I'm sure it's not her!"

"She is, she is! She certainly is! And all these parcels are for her, right? Well, I will help you get there. Do you know where Lătești is? Do you know how to get there?"

"No, I don't. I was thinking about taking a cab."

"You will find no cab and even if you do, no cab driver would take you there. In order to get to Lătești we'll have to take a bus; the village is quite far away. Listen to me, I go there too and I know the way. I will help you, don't worry!" she added. She seemed to have already decided for me. We were going together to Lătești, and there was nothing else to be said.

The woman never left my side. She stood next to me all along the trip. She didn't have to go back to her compartment because she had no luggage.

"From the train station in Fetești to the bus station," she added, "it's not far, but we still need help to carry all these parcels. I will ask a few people to give us a hand." She kept talking, so I didn't have a chance to say anything.

Once we arrived in Fetești she called to a few young fellows, "Hey, you there, would you be so nice as to help us?"

We got on a bus with all that luggage, and it started jolting along the bumpy rough road. It was dark inside and there were no lights along the road. I had no idea where we were heading. The woman told me, "From the bus station to the house of the priest's wife it's quite a long way to go. It would not be hard to get there if we didn't have any luggage, but with all these parcels we'll need help. But don't you worry; I'll ask some of those who get off there to give us a hand. We need help," she added with her typical optimism.

And so it was. I have no idea how many people got off there; all I remember was that the woman and I were carrying the heavy suitcase by holding the ends of a thick stick we had put through its handles. We were walking in the moonlight. I was exhausted and kept on stumbling in all the holes in the road. I wished I could put the suitcase down and rest for a little while, but my companion kept on encouraging me, "There's just a little bit more. You can do it; we are almost there."

Then she would turn to the people helping us carry the rest of the luggage and say, "Walk in silence, not to wake up the dogs—they would tear us to pieces!"

We finally arrived in Lătești, "the misery village". The woman stopped in front of the house (or more like the clay hut) I was looking for and said, "This is where the pastor's wife lives." I took a few steps forward and saw the children in the dim light of the lamp. I turned to my companion to express my gratitude and thank her, to take the luggage and invite her inside, to introduce her to the family. But when I looked back over my shoulder she was no longer there. All I could see were the parcels left there in the road. She had vanished in the night. Everything seemed to have vanished. I looked all around me trying to find my mysterious companion, but there was no trace of her. I thought, "That's OK, Iuliana and Marica will help me find her tomorrow; they must know her since she lives here."

I entered the hut and met the Viski family. I will never forget those moments. The image of the five boys and two girls in that little clay hut will stay in my memory forever. A blanket separated the "bedroom" from the "kitchen". The walls and floor were made of clay. Rows of wooden planks stretched from one "bedroom" wall to the other, forming a makeshift bunk bed for all the kids: Francisc, Ștefan, Paul, Lidia, Hughi, Peter and Andrei. The little ones had a teddy bear, and that night (at least for the few hours that were left of it) I had the honor of sleeping between two of the children and their toy.

The house in Lătești

They were so happy to see me! First of all they were excited to meet somebody from outside their "prison", and secondly they rejoiced seeing God's love and provision for them in the gift He had sent through me. They were celebrating Easter the

The Viski family

following day, and the Lord wanted them to do it cheerfully. I was His gift for them, and our hearts were joined together forever in His holy love.

Next morning I tried to find out who the woman from the train was. When I described her to Iuliana and Marica they looked at each other and said, "No one here looks like that."

"But how about the piano lessons?" I asked them, completely confused.

"Piano lessons? In the desolate Bărăgan Plain? Here, in Lătești?"

Then I understood that we are never alone. Our Lord has suffered the agony all by Himself but we are never alone or forsaken. Oh, Lord, open the eyes of our heart so we may see and believe

Tea with No Sugar

In my sophomore year I had another remarkable experience. Dad was still in prison because he had been sentenced to six years. Mom's salary had to cover all our needs as well as Dad's monthly food parcels. Oftentimes we could barely make it from month to month. One day, Mom told me she had the chance to go on a ten day vacation for free at a holiday resort. Working in a radiology department, she was exposed on a regular basis to radiations that could damage her health. She agreed to go, thinking it would save the money for her food if she left for ten days.

She gave me some money for food and she left. Two days later I was already missing her and feeling kind of lonely. One fall afternoon I had finished my lab practice and was wondering where to go. There was nobody home, I had no more food or money, and I was hungry. I decided to go visit Brother Ioanid and sister Leana, thinking they might invite me to stay for dinner. I was always welcome in their home and they were as close to me as my own parents, especially since Dad had been imprisoned. They were glad to see me, indeed. We talked from the Scripture, we recited some poems, talked about our families, but nothing about dinner. I finally stood up to go home and they walked me to the door.

Embarrassed, they said to me, "Dear Puşa, we would have liked to have dinner together, but we have nothing to eat tonight. We'll just drink a cup of tea with no sugar."

"That's all right," I said as I left.

When you're young, you don't pay much attention to such things. I was hungry indeed, but I was glad I could save some money for my father's food parcel. At least I was free. I went home and got ready for bed. Around ten o'clock I heard the dog barking outside. It always warned us when someone was coming. I was a little bit afraid, not knowing who could have come at such a late hour, especially now when I was home alone. A few moments later somebody knocked on our door.

"Who is it?" I asked.

"Puşa, it's me, Sister Aglaia. Please open the door."

Bewildered, I hurried to the door and asked, "What happened, sister Aglaia, to make you come all the way here at this late hour?"

She lived quite far from us. It took her a while to get to us by tram, plus about half an hour of walking.

"Dear Puşa, I cooked some rice with milk, and the thought of bringing some to you would not leave me alone. So here I am, with a bowl of warm food for you. I'm glad I got here in time, before you went to bed!"

You can easily imagine how touched I was. Of course I could have gone to sleep on an empty tummy. Of course I would have been content even with sister Leana's tea. But the Lord wanted to show me a sign of His love and sent Sister Aglaia just in time to bring me my favorite food—rice with milk. I considered her food a holy gift, and her kindness is a precious memory I will treasure for the rest of my life.

My Graduation Exam

My final academic year came quickly. I had to study a lot and graduation exams were just around the corner. I hadn't been able to focus enough on school. I'd been distracted by legal undertakings on behalf of my father (which I had attempted just to keep my conscience clear, not because I trusted the authorities to do us justice), and by our material needs. I began studying really hard but could not see myself passing those exams. The one that really worried me was Physical Chemistry. I hadn't been able to understand that class from the very beginning. It seemed more than I could handle, and I was terrified thinking I would be examined by the most demanding professor. Humanly speaking, I felt hopeless.

The day before the exam I tried to memorize some formulas, but it didn't help. The afternoon before that dreadful exam I was sitting at my desk with tens of pages full of notes, but my head was empty. Telling myself it was too late anyway, I decided to go to a group meeting. Maybe that would help me calm down so I'd be able to study more later. I returned quite late, but I was not that scared anymore. It was impossible to keep on studying at that late hour. I went to sleep and next morning reality hit me: exam time! I was terrified. What was I going to do?

"Lord, please help me. I know I don't deserve it because I didn't study hard enough, but I didn't understand that class anyway . . ."

Getting on my knees to pray before going to the university, like I used to do every day, I opened my Bible to read a passage. My eyes fell on the following verse: "Joseph found favor in his eyes . . ." That verse was addressed to me.

I didn't need anything else. I closed the Bible and said, "Thank You, my Lord. Just as Joseph found favor in Egypt, I will find favor at this exam."

Rejoicing, I ran to the university. But there was nothing to rejoice about. The professor had been failing students one after another and seemed disgusted by our stupidity. The students entered two by two, and each one would pick a piece of paper with a certain topic from a box. The professor expected the students' presentations to have a certain logic, but none of them seemed able to reach his standard. He was indignant, and so were the students.

When I arrived, the atmosphere was really tense. The door opened and a student as pale as a ghost came from inside. He had failed, and the professor told him how he should have presented his topic in order to pass. That student told us what the professor would have liked to hear, and he was upset because such an approach had never crossed his mind.

When it was my turn to enter the examination hall I picked a piece of paper with the topic I was going to present. I sat down and read the title.

Closing my eyes I saw God's face smiling down on me. I had picked the same topic my schoolmate had just explained in detail. I felt like laughing and crying for joy at the same time.

The professor was more than pleased to finally find someone who was able to present that topic with such logic and clarity.

I felt like Joseph in Egypt, just as I had read that morning from the Bible. Now I thanked and praised my living and true God!

This is how, by God's grace, I graduated from the Chemistry Faculty of the Bucharest University.

This event called for a celebration, of course, so we held a meeting in our home, inviting all who had prayed for me. I would have dropped out of school long ago, but my brothers and sisters (especially Brother Caraman and Brother Ioanid) convinced me not to give up. They kept me in their prayers, encouraged me, and supported me financially. They were our advisors, our brothers and our friends.

We rejoiced and celebrated my graduation together, singing songs and reciting poems.

Ministry in the Villages

In those days I used to ride my bike to the churches in the neighboring villages, with Brother Caraman and Brother Ioanid. All three of us were tall and skinny. We used to sing as loud as we could when there were no houses along the road. Once, a few days before going to a village I got an allergy and my skin started itching badly. What had happened? Never had I had such problems before. However, I didn't want to miss this chance to serve the Lord. Before leaving I put on warm clothes to make sure I wouldn't be cold. I didn't feel well at all and my skin was itching even worse because of the bike riding.

Before arriving in the village we rode through a forest and stopped in a little glade to rest for a while. Brother Caraman suggested we should pray for my allergy. I accepted gladly, of course. We prayed, and the Lord healed me. After that we went our way singing joyfully. Brother Caraman's sister, Caliopi, used to come by bus while Sister Leana, Brother Ioanid's wife, could not come at all. She had a heart condition (though she had a very big heart). What great memories!

God inspired Brother Ioanid to write poem after poem, and we took them from church to church. I felt like the Apostle Paul, who was brought up at the feet of Gamaliel. It was as if I was living heaven on earth. I was in love with my Lord and I also loved poetry, given my interest for drama. Brother Ioanid had been an actor and he taught me how to recite his poems.

A Very Special Train Excursion

Knowing I would soon need to get a job, I decided to travel roundtrip by train through Romania with Victorița, a good friend of mine. We chose a few places where we would spend one or more days, then continue our trip until we arrived back where we had started from. Our train ticket had to be stamped both when we got off in a train station, and when we got on the train again. The roundtrip ticket included a few stops, so it was cheaper than a regular ticket.

We decided to stop in towns where we had friends so we could spend the night. We were so excited. Our first stop was in Brașov, a picturesque mountain town. In the neighborhood we could visit medieval castles, fir-tree forests, glades filled with fragrant daffodils—but best of all, dear families of believers. The Bunica family was my favorite.

I had met Eva while I was still a university student, during one of the practice periods, in one of the nearby factories. She had become my friend and our relationship was going to last forever. When God's love unites people, nothing can separate them.

Our visit there was extremely pleasant. Sister Bunica, who was an excellent cook, gave us some food supplies for our trip.

We were joyful and had a huge feeling of relief knowing we were done with our exams; we were admiring God's creation and felt as if the places we saw belonged to us. They had been created by our Father, so they were ours too. The flowers were my sisters and the trees my brothers. The animals seemed able to understand me so I would say a meow, a moo or a baa when we passed by them. I wasn't so sure about the dogs and the way they would react so I left them alone as long as they didn't bother me.

The Bunica family

This is how we arrived up North in Bucovina. Our destination was the village of Pătrăuți where we intended to visit Brother Vasile Răscol, a well-known prophet of God. In my first years when I started to study and learn from the Bible, I found out that God was not merely an idea or a myth. He was a real Person whose divine qualities surpass our understanding. We as humans don't have the ability to comprehend Him completely, though we were created in his own likeness and image. But Jesus who is still alive today is talking to us. He knows everything because He is all-knowing, and sometimes—when it is for our good—He chooses to reveal to us things we otherwise could not know.

The people He chooses to reveal His (or our) mysteries to are called prophets, and Brother Vasile Răscol, Sr. was one of them. Going to a prayer meeting where he was present was quite a privilege, and one we enjoyed quite rarely. He lived in Bucovina, 500 km away from Bucharest. Still we knew him because most of his children had moved to Bucharest and two of them were part of my church. So we got to see him when he came to visit his children. To our pleasant surprise, in brother Răscol's house we found Vasile Jr., his son. Though part of the same church, we hadn't yet been acquainted, because we were in different small fellowship groups.

Bistrița Bârgăului: Village in the Meadow

We went from Pătrăuți to Bistrița Bârgăului, where a gathering of believers from different villages were planning to celebrate a special event.

Bistrița Bârgăului

Josenii Bârgăului was a small mountain village. I had been invited by Sister Olguța Șmilovici who had come there from Bucharest.

The gathering was held in a cottage surrounded by meadows full of flowers. Dressed in their picturesque traditional costumes the believers started coming over the hills, singing all along the way. To me the atmosphere seemed part of a fairytale. The women had baked fresh bread and pies, and had cooked cabbage rolls and other kinds of goodies. We were all waiting for the evening when we were planning to gather together for prayer. What could be better than that? The atmosphere was like heaven.

We were already there when brothers Victor and Vasile Răscol Jr. arrived riding a motorbike. That's when I realized I had forgotten to have my ticket stamped at the train station. I would have to go back there by bus, so when I saw the motorbike I took the opportunity and asked Victor if he could do me a favor and take me there. The idea of riding the motorbike seemed like a real adventure to me!

"Sister Pușa," he said to me, "I'd help you gladly if I weren't so exhausted, but I believe my brother Vasile would be happy to take you there."

Vasile riding his motobike

I didn't care who took me there as long as I got to the train station; besides, the idea of riding the motorbike seemed very appealing.

I didn't have to ask Vasile twice. He was probably even more tired than his brother Victor since he had been driving the motorbike, but he didn't mind taking a young lady for a ride.

And so we set off riding the motorbike on the rough country roads, passing through picturesque villages while being refreshed by the cool air. The trip seemed too short, so we chose a different itinerary on the way back. However, we made sure it would not take too long because we had to be back in time for a hike we had planned; we were going to climb the surrounding hills and pick wild raspberries.

Our large group was spread over several glades and hills, but still not too far apart to sing our favorite Christian songs together. It was a lovely time, especially for me, a city girl, who hadn't had many chances to enjoy the beauty of the outdoors. I had no idea how Vasile managed to pick raspberries so fast and bring them to me. I wasn't that skillful. However I ate them all and didn't intend to share.

That afternoon we returned to our host, the Holbură family. The women were all busy cooking dinner so I went outside. I could not get enough of that fresh air. The scent of the freshly cut grass was wonderful. I had never breathed such delightful air in Bucharest. Vasile followed me outside and we sat next to each other leaning on a hay stack.

National costumes

Hay stacks

We felt as if we were in our Father's yard. Vasile asked me about my life and how I came to know the Lord. Of all the stories I could tell, that was my favorite one. I was in love with my Lord Jesus and I could not hide that, my thankfulness or my enthusiasm. We talked until later that evening. It was getting chilly but none of us dared to move for fear we might put an end to those beautiful moments together. Sister Olguța brought us a blanket. It was getting dark and it was time to go inside.

Next morning I got a telegram from my mom asking me to return home right away. I had been assigned to a job at a pharmaceutical factory in Bucharest and was expected there as soon as possible. I said goodbye to everyone and Vasile gave me a ride on his motorbike to the train station. We had become friends, and something in my heart was telling me our relationship was not going to end there. When we arrived at the train station he bought me a chocolate; I hadn't had such a treat in a long, long time. When we parted we promised each other we would meet again in church. On my way back to Bucharest I relived everything I had experienced in that short but beautiful vacation. Still there was a trace of sadness in my heart because I could not share my joy with Dad. I realized it was not fair for me to be so happy while he was imprisoned, but I was happy, and I had peace in my heart.

The Vial Pharmaceutical Factory

I could have been assigned a job somewhere out in the countryside because there were few jobs in Bucharest, and those were only for those with relations in high circles. As for me, I must have had relations in the "highest possible circle" to get a job in the capital.

After quite a short time I started working at the Vial Pharmaceutical Factory in Bucharest. As a chemical engineer I had to supervise the manufacturing and the packaging of medicines. It was a difficult task requiring special attention not to place the substances in the wrong vial. It would have been a disaster to pack morphine in distilled water vials. One mistake might cause the death of one or more persons.

The police were always surveying our activity in order to make sure no one was stealing any drugs or narcotics. I started working at 6 a.m. and finished when the workers on the afternoon shift arrived. Sometimes I would work on the afternoon shift and return home after midnight. My superior was a real shrew, but youth often disregards such hardships.

~ PART FOUR ~
True Love

Preoccupied with Vasile

I started thinking about Vasile all the time. I could hardly wait for the Sundays when we would meet in church. When the service was over and people hung around talking, I pretended to be engaged in conversation with other believers or to be busy doing something, but I did not let Vasile out of my sight. I don't know how come, but he kept his eyes on me too, and I loved it.

Like any other girl I had often thought about marriage and my wedding day. All I wanted was a genuine believer for a husband. However, I wished he were good looking and dark haired too. I would have never wanted a blond. All those thoughts that kept swarming in my mind made me smile.

Whenever I prayed about marriage I used to say, "Lord, how can I know which young man is the one You've chosen for me? How can I be sure he is the person with whom I can work out my salvation?"

It was an important decision for me because I knew it had lifelong implications. I didn't want to choose the wrong marriage partner and realize afterwards that I had been mistaken. Like my fellow believers I did not consider divorce an option, so I needed to be certain that my choice reflected God's will. Therefore, I prayed, "God, please give me a sign and make it easier for me to discern. When a young man proposes I will ask him if he is convinced that's God's will for us. If his answer is a categorical yes, I will know it is him. But if he hesitates or is uncertain, I will know I should not accept his proposal."

My request was simple and logical, so I was now waiting to see what

Vasile and me

was going to happen. As time went by, several young men proposed, but when I asked them the key question they gave me evasive answers that showed me very clearly they were not meant for me. So I thanked God for His guidance and went on.

Flowers from Vasile

One evening we held a prayer meeting in our house. It was a special occasion celebrating my birthday. We always took advantage of such occasions to validate our gatherings, in case the Secret Police discovered us. Vasile was there too. He had not been part of my fellowship group, but after we got to know each other in Bistriţa he enjoyed joining us. That night he brought me flowers for my birthday. As everyone knows, flowers symbolize something and they send a message to the one who receives them. If a young man gives a girl a bunch of red roses she will know he loves her. Vasile brought me some white callas, the symbol of marriage. I didn't know what to think when he gave me the flowers. I looked at him, but he was shy and uneasy, and didn't seem to realize the meaning of his gift. I thanked him and smiled. Was it just a coincidence? Vasile was good looking and dark haired but . . . I didn't want to let my imagination run wild.

We kept on seeing each other. He would come to see me often, and a strong friendship began to connect the two of us. We couldn't wait to meet again. He was an introvert while I was very talkative. I felt he enjoyed seeing and listening to me. His timidity attracted me because I was sick and tired of the frivolous, audacious and cheeky non-believing young men I had met around me. Though I liked Vasile I was still cautious. I wanted to give my heart only to the one who was going to be my husband, so I was waiting to hear his answer to the key question I was going to ask him. One night, when my shift was over, Vasile came to walk me home. He didn't want me to go all by myself when it was dark outside. On the way home he started telling me shyly that he wanted to spend the rest of his life with me. So I asked him why.

"Because I care about you," his answer came. He didn't have the courage to tell me that he loved me.

For me that was a defining moment and I was quite nervous. I asked him the big question. "But do you believe that is God's will for us?"

He kept silent for a moment while my heart was racing. Then, with a husky but certain voice he answered, "I would not have dared to ask you to spend the rest of your life with me if I weren't convinced God approved of our relationship."

A thrill went through my heart, and I felt God's Spirit was assuring me Vasile's answer was not a mere coincidence. He was God's chosen for me.

I was so happy—not only because Vasile was the one, but because of the feeling of trust I had in the One who had become very real to me. His strong, sweet presence revealed Him to me as a loving and caring Father. Besides my dad, I also had a heavenly Father who was by my side.

People often ask, "How do you know God is real? How do you know He exists and that He loves you?" Such questions are reasonable when we know God is Spirit—a power we are afraid might crush us. But when you are His child, when He becomes your Father by faith, then you know it. You can't explain this experience; you can only live it. Does a child need someone to prove the authenticity of his father? He simply knows his dad is his dad. He doesn't need any explanation or proof.

When I looked Vasile in the eyes we both knew a secret that didn't need to be expressed. God had created us for each other and He had woven the thread of our lives together in the tapestry of His plan. But what kind of plan did He have in mind? What was His purpose for us? None of us knew the answer back then, but we were certain we were His and that was enough.

I did not answer Vasile's question right away, but I knew without a doubt that I would tell him "Yes."

Engagement in the Forest

The celebration of Communist Workers' Day was an event everybody was waiting for, not because it represented something precious for the people but because we had two days off. On the 1st of May, Romanians had to participate in the parade organized for the Communist Party, proving their loyalty to the regime by chanting slogans and singing songs of praise for the party. But we could spend the following day the way we chose to.

May was the month of flowers and new hopes. The rays of the sun warmed us and the sweet scent of flowers delighted us. After the long, cold winter, spring was like a beautiful dream.

Since we both had a day off we decided to take a walk in Băneasa forest. It was a popular refuge from the jostle of the city. We held hands while walking in search of a secluded, picturesque spot. We started recounting our lives to each other. Vasile knew many details about my life, so now it was my turn to listen to him and try to understand this man the Lord had brought into my life—the man I loved dearly, though I didn't know very much about him. I wanted to find out more so I started with a question. "How did you get the assurance that the Lord has made us for each other?"

His words amazed me.

Engagement in the forest

"A long time ago I started asking the Lord in my prayers to give me a wife who would help me remain faithful to Him for as long as I shall live. That was my only request. I didn't ask for riches or beauty, but only for faithfulness to the Lord. Time passed by, so I intensified my prayer. I decided to start fasting too, and one night I had a dream. I saw myself standing on a hill; in front of me there was another hill and you were standing there. As soon as we saw each other we opened our arms, we ran, we met, and we embraced each other in the valley between those hills. I liked you from the moment I laid eyes on you, and that feeling got stronger every day."

I was struggling to control my emotions. The gentleness of his words had charmed me. While we kept on walking we came across a glade filled with wild flowers. Butterflies were flying from flower to flower and the birds were chirping all around us. We sat somewhere in the shade. Vasile started picking wild flowers and making a wreath. When he was done he brought it to me, put it on my head and asked, "How about getting engaged right here, in the middle of God's creation?"

We were both overwhelmed by the deep feelings of love we had for each other, and for our heavenly Father as well. We made wedding rings out of the flowers we plucked from the glade and I already had a flower wreath on my head. We summoned heaven and earth as witnesses, held each other's hands in prayer and promised we would be together for the rest of our lives. We made a strong, serious covenant right then and there. We also kissed for the first time.

Once Again in Bărăgan

We set our wedding day for the seventh day of the seventh month (July 7), the perfect number. However, this was only after we went to see my father together and asked for his blessing.

I wished that long road through the plain of Bărăgan did not exist on the world's map. That road separated me from the one who had given me life and who had brought me to the Lord through his prayers. It was a road I didn't want to travel anymore, though I knew I had to. Once I set off I wished it would never end, because at the end of that road a painful meeting was waiting for me, a meeting I both longed for and tried to postpone as much as possible. How could I explain my mixed feelings? I wanted to see my beloved dad but I didn't want to see him there. I wished it was only a nightmare I would wake up from, relieved to see it was gone. But it was not just a bad dream.

This time Vasile accompanied me when I went to see my father. Mom had already approved of our marriage and we were going to ask now for Dad's blessing as well.

Stories from Vasile's Childhood

On the way to the labor camp we started talking. "Please tell me about your childhood," I asked him.

"Oh, my childhood was an ordinary one; there's nothing special about it."

"Still, tell me. I'm interested to hear about it."

Vasile's family

"I was the eighth child in our family. My parents were born-again believers when I was born, but they hadn't been like that before. My mother was the first one who received the faith, and my father allowed her to go to church. Soon after she came to Christ, my dad's unbeliever friends started telling him, 'How can you allow your wife to go in that place where the devil is hiding under the table, while the people there do all kinds of iniquities?'

"So my father decided to go and see for himself if those charges were true. He put on some nice clothes and one day he went to church. The believers there welcomed him and invited him to sit on the first row. He sat down and waited to see what would happen. To his surprise, he heard the speakers explaining the Bible, and he felt that all of them were reading his mind. The Holy Spirit touched his heart and from that day on he went to church with my mom.

"When I was born, my older brothers and sisters had already left our village, but you know that part of the story."

I knew it but I wanted to find out more.

And so Vasile kept on telling his story. "Victor, Mircea and Lenuța were already gone. The next one was Ionel, my brother who had some health issues; he was followed by a girl, Lidia. I was the next born, and the last two were Viorica and Neculai. They were too small so I helped mom with everything, except for Lidia's household duties. Since Dad was a pastor and a prophet, he was gone most of the time. I remember the prayer meetings that took place often in our house. I would wake up and go to bed surrounded by prayers. Before the believers in the neighborhood began their daily chores, they would pass by to bring thanks to God for a new day. On Sundays we would always have guests. My mother (Sister Ghena) used to cook in large pots and she invited the fellow believers from other villages who were visiting us to stay for dinner. They left their carriages in our yard and I fetched water for their horses. My sisters set the table, and dinner would start and end with prayer."

While listening to his beautiful life story I realized it was quite different from mine. Sometimes I told myself Vasile was so blessed to be born and raised in such a wonderful atmosphere, but then I thought twice and was deeply grateful to God for my own life and the way He had brought me into His house as well.

Vasile continued telling me about his childhood and I could picture myself in those vivid images of his past, joining him in his field work, pulling the weeds, reaping the harvest or giving water to the animals.

"In the fall, after harvesting the corn, the villagers would carry it home and then gather together to help each other manually remove the corn kernels. One evening they would go to one villager's house, the next evening in somebody else's, until all the work was done. They usually invited the storyteller of the village as well to tell some stories, so that those moments were pleasant and appealing for the children, too. The telling of one story lasted for several evenings. They weren't printed in any books, but had been handed down orally from one generation to the next."

"Please tell me one of those stories," I asked Vasile.

"Some other time," he replied. "They are too long and I don't remember them well. We should ask Neculai to do that."

"Then when are we going to invite him over?"

Vasile just smiled.

The Waiting Room

We both arrived at the labor camp's waiting room; it was dirty, smelly and full of flies. The food parcel did not seem so heavy this time because we carried it together. But the heaviness in my heart was more difficult to bear.

We joined the other visitors who waited for their loved ones to return from their daily labor. Vasile was shocked. He saw for the first time in his life the long line of exhausted prisoners who returned to the camp dragging their feet through the dust on the road, with their heads bowed and the shovels on their shoulders. He had read about such scenes in Tolstoi's or Dostoievski's novels, but this was the first time he saw that reality with his own eyes.

My father saw us from afar. He raised his shovel for a few times as a sign he had seen us. No doubt he was wondering who the young man standing next to his daughter was.

He tried to stay behind, allowing others to take his place in line, to gain a few more moments of eye contact. All the prisoners entered through the gates that were closed with a loud bang behind them.

We had to wait now for our turn to spend a few moments with Dad. Vasile was not allowed to enter with me, but at least dad had the chance to see him.

When I met Dad I told him about Vasile and I asked him if he agreed with our marriage. With tears in his eyes he replied, "If you love each other, you have my blessing. The fact that he is the son of Brother Vasile Răscol, Sr. is a good enough guarantee for me."

Wedding Preparations

We all wished Dad could come to our wedding, but he still had to spend many years in prison.

For most of the people who were not subservient to the communist regime, money was a major problem in those days. My family, however, was not concerned with the issue of money or material things. Vasile shared the same beliefs.

We often talked about our aspirations. This is how we got to know each other better. We were so different from each other—almost completely different. Maybe that's why we were so attracted to one another. But the one thing we had in common was more important than our differences; it was our love, devotion and trust in the Lord Jesus. He was involved in all our decisions. We both wanted to be useful for His kingdom.

The wedding day was getting closer and we were busy preparing for that event.

Firica, a good friend of my mother, was going to make my bridal gown. She was an excellent dressmaker, and besides, she loved me as if I were her own daughter. That dress was her wedding gift for me.

The wedding reception was another problem. Food was expensive and scarce—money too—while the guests would be many. We were both known in the congregations in our cities, and usually lots of brothers and sisters participated in wedding ceremonies. Weddings were real celebrations with songs, poems and good preachers. There were flowers, joy and afterwards food for everyone. For that custom of offering food for everyone we needed a solution. And the solution came from the only One who could provide it, our heavenly Father. Vasile's family from Pătrăuți sent Neculai to bring us some veal, which was truly a royal gift in those times. My mom and some other sisters in our congregation cooked it. They also baked cakes, and how tasty those cakes were! Sister Leana, Brother Ioanid's wife, made the wedding cake—a great cake, decorated by her husband. For a beverage, we had plenty of water.

Another problem was, where would we live after the wedding? My mom and I lived in two rented rooms where Dad was going to return after he served his time in prison. Those two rooms were bedroom, living room, bathroom and kitchen. There was no way Vasile and I could move in there. He lived in a garret with a small roof window. To get in he had to climb a narrow spiral staircase. In his tiny room in the attic there was a bed, a closet and a stove he used to warm that place and sometimes to cook. But being young, he did not realize the drawbacks. That was where we were going to live together.

We were living in a socialist country where all homes were owned by the state. In order to receive a place to stay we had to fill in a form after we got married and then wait—maybe for years—until something became available. Since we were not members of the Communist Party it was obvious we were not going to be given priority, and we were very realistic about our chances.

Once, when I was only a child, I dreamt I would live in an apartment with running water, a bathroom and a kitchen, like my brother Valentin. Now I understood the situation better, and I did not have such dreams anymore. I was trying to enjoy what we did have. And we had a lot: our life and freedom, a job that provided enough money to survive, but above everything else we had God. On top of that, we now (almost) had each other, and because of this positive outlook on life the attic room did not seem so small anymore. Many would have liked to have what we did.

The neighborhood I grew up in was a Jewish one. One of our neighbors, Mrs. Schwarz, was a very wise lady from whom I learned not to complain. Sometimes she went through great hardships too. When I asked her, "How are you doing, Mrs. Schwarz?" she would answer, "I could do better." She never said she was doing badly, but only that things could be better. We could have done better too, but we were not complaining.

The Milan Family and Aunt Dora

One day, when Vasile and I went to visit Sister Binția, she told us, "My dear children, you will get married soon, and you have no place to stay. I thought you could live in the Milans' apartment. You know the family. They applied for permission to immigrate to Israel, but only the Milans got approval; Aunt Dora didn't. They occupy a two-bedroom apartment in Cotroceni. After they leave the country, the state will surely assign the free room to someone else to share the apartment with Aunt Dora. If you want, I can talk to her so that you can move in there right after the Milans leave. If Aunt Dora accepts, it will be more difficult for the authorities to kick you out of there."

My heart started beating faster and my mind could already picture the scenario. I had visited the Milans a short time ago and I remembered how wonderful the neighborhood was and how comfortable their apartment. There were two rooms—one larger and the other smaller. From the larger room one could enter the bathroom. There was hot water like in Valentin's apartment. There also was gas heating, a small kitchen, an entrance hall and a pantry. It truly was a dream. Maybe Aunt Dora would allow us to stay in the smaller room and keep the larger one for herself...

Calm down, girl; don't let your mind run wild. It's just a thoughtful suggestion, a good idea, a way Sister Binția is showing her love for you, I told myself.

But Sister Binția was not the kind of person who only talked. She took action, too. Aunt Dora didn't know us, but she had known Sister Binția for a lifetime and appreciated her greatly. So, she accepted us for her friend's sake.

Only days remained until the departure of the Milans and we had to act quickly. Someone could be assigned to occupy that room at any moment, but we were not married yet. Sister Binția decided Vasile was

Our civil marriage ceremony

to move in there immediately. There were two more weeks until our marriage day. Sister Binția and Mom helped us carry over a few pieces of furniture so the room would not remain empty.

Aunt Dora told us, "Children, I'll stay in the small room I've stayed in all along. You'll take the larger one since you are two; just let me use the bathroom when I need to."

That was way too much! Did she really mean it? She was willing to share her apartment with us, and she was asking for our permission to use her own bathroom? We were overwhelmed.

Of course, the city hall sent their agents to assign the available room to someone, but Aunt Dora told them that a young couple had just moved in and that she had agreed. The living space department asked us to present our marriage certificate at their office by the 5th of July.

Our civil marriage ceremony was on July 4. The sequence of those events proved once more our heavenly Father's provision. The departure of the Milans on the eve of our marriage, Sister Binția's idea, Aunt Dora's kindness, and God's wedding gift for us were certainly not mere coincidences.

We were not going to live in an attic, but in one of the most beautiful districts of Bucharest. In fact, the apartment was part of a three floor villa. The whole building had been confiscated by the state, which allocated the apartments to different families, according to the number of members. By state law each person could be allocated a maximum of ten square meters so Vasile could not have had the larger room to himself, for it required at least two persons. Vasile didn't dare go out too often for fear of being kicked out of that apartment.

We were nervous, even though we understood it was God's will for us to be there. Nothing could go wrong because He was watching over us.

Aunt Dora was a very kind elderly woman, weakened because of physical suffering. She was like a grandmother to me. In the few days before our wedding she had already grown accustomed to Vasile. I believe he fully won her over when he tried to cook some cheese dumplings for her. (I didn't dare to ask her if she liked them.)

Our Wedding Day

On our wedding day, Ionel rented a cab to take us to church, then to a photographer, then to give us a ride through the city, and then take us home. We felt truly pampered.

Dressed as a bride, I was coming from my mother's place. Vasile, my handsome groom, was coming from "our place".

When we arrived at church, the building was full of people. The hall could not fit everyone, so many people stood in the yard, even on the street. I had chosen the largest church building for the wedding, but it was still too small. The gathering of so many dear brothers and sisters was touching. We could hardly get inside. Everyone wanted to see us, to touch us.

The bride and groom at the photographer's

When we stepped inside we stopped for a moment to make sure the one who would officiate our marriage ceremony was the brother we'd chosen and not one delegated by the authorities, according to the communist rules of those times. When we saw that Brother Emil Bulgăr was there we headed to our places. It was Sunday morning, July 7, 1963.

After the service ended at 1:00 p.m., the reception was ready at my mom's place. There were large tables in the house and the yard. We could sing and rejoice together without fear. It was a wedding day, after all . . . Or so we thought.

At our wedding I had invited a friend from Cluj, Piri Fărăgău. She had brought her missionary uncle Gulyas (or Pişta, as he was called), who was visiting from America, the motherland of capitalism so hated by communists. America was portrayed as a country where people ate garbage and were killing each other on the streets, a place where a handful of rich people were exploiting the rest.

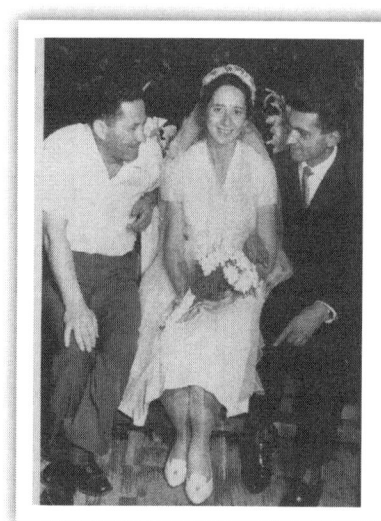

Pista and us, and the wedding guests

That was the image of America the Communist propaganda conveyed, however, all who wanted to be free dreamed of getting there.

We were honored and happy to have a missionary from America at our wedding. Yet we had no idea what trials would follow after that. We would find out pretty soon.

That night after everyone left, we said goodbye to my mother and went to our apartment.

Poor Mother, I'm sure she cried. She was alone for the first time after my father's arrest. I had been with her and comforted her for so long.

Now I had left the nest, moving into the beautiful apartment in Cotroceni where we had a toilet and a bathroom, a wooden floor, a kitchen and a pantry. My childhood dream was being fulfilled. Part of it was coming true right then. The other parts of my dream were to marry a man who had a car, and to be able to travel abroad. It was like dreaming I would fly to the moon. Who could have had a car and permission to travel abroad without being a member of the Communist Party? That part of my dream seemed impossible.

I forgot to mention that our street, Dr. Mirunescu Street, had lime trees on both sides, and when they were in bloom they dispersed a wonderful fragrance.

Our wedding celebration was too beautiful to remain unnoticed by the communist authorities. It was too beautiful not to arouse hatred in the minds of those whose father was the devil—hatred and suspicion. Since they didn't have the Lord, how could they understand the inner peace and happiness of those who turned to God's love and forgiveness? We had had a simple but blessed wedding. But trials don't knock on the door to ask if they are welcome. They come when you least expect them, as we were about to see for ourselves.

~ PART FIVE ~
Complications

The Secret Police

We lived under the brutal dictatorship of the Secret Police. Most people were horrified by the specter of political prisons and labor camps, which killed both physically and morally. Those were indeed terrible times for Romania.

The Secret Police agents came to our door and asked us to go to their office. So many thoughts whirled in our heads. I remembered my father's arrest and my heart started racing. We heard that brothers Constantin Caraman and Gașpar Vasile had been summoned to the Secret Police headquarters and arrested in the meantime.

What crime had we committed? We would find out soon. The Secret Police agents wanted to know what that American citizen was doing at our wedding. What was the subversive purpose of his visit? We had hosted a capitalist spy at our wedding. To whom had he talked? What had he said? What intrigues was he up to?

These were the questions we were summoned to answer for days on end, week after week.

I had to give statement after statement. But we had nothing to tell. We were asked the same questions endlessly, in hopes we would fall into their trap and certify their suppositions.

Other dear brothers and sisters who came to our wedding were arrested as well. We could ease the pain and concern for their safety only through prayer. *We prayed, Lord, this is our time of trial. We are mere people, but we are Yours. Help us and our brethren.*

I was pregnant with our first child, but the Secret Police did not care. Their mission was to rule using terror as an effective tool. They sought to keep the entire country at their feet through intimidation and terror.

"What did Pişta say to your wedding guests in the back yard?"

"Comrade, do you know what my role was at the wedding?" I asked in reply.

"You were the bride."

"And where did I sit?"

"With the groom at the table."

"Then how should I know what people were saying outside, in the courtyard?"

"Come on, don't try to be clever with us; it's not going to work!"

Day after day I could see and feel the Lord's help. I used to pray and read Scripture before going to the Secret Police Headquarters for interrogation. Each time a Bible verse would encourage me, such as Psalm 94:

> When I said, "My foot is slipping," your unfailing love, LORD, supported me. When anxiety was great within me, your consolation brought me joy. Can a corrupt throne be allied with you—a throne that brings on misery by its decrees? The wicked band together against the righteous and condemn the innocent to death. But the LORD has become my fortress, and my God the rock in whom I take refuge. He will repay them for their sins and destroy them for their wickedness; the LORD our God will destroy them.

It was our time to prove our faithfulness and to believe the Word of God as it is written in Hebrew 11:1: "Now faith is the substance of things hoped for, the evidence of things not seen." Only in such circumstances could His promises prove to be true. "Your unfailing love, Lord, supported me." We had to believe that truth even in the midst of adversities and threats. When we did that, we saw the Word of God being fulfilled in our lives.

After a while things calmed down a little. Our fellow believers were released from prison because the authorities had no proof to incriminate them. Of course they did not apologize for all the trouble they had caused.

In the meantime, Aunt Dora received approval to immigrate in Israel, and she left the country. Since we were expecting a child, we received permission to occupy the smaller room as well, so the entire apartment was now ours.

Children's Ministry

Life went on. The gatherings of the body of Christ were our joy. We were involved in the children's ministry in our congregation. It was a pleasure to see the children coming in good or bad weather, happy that someone cared for them, eager to learn, help, play, and eat some sweets at the end of the lesson, which usually took place in our home. We took plenty advantage of the large room in our apartment. .

The children had lots of energy. We organized them by age groups. Filip Dembi was the assistant for the older kids' group; then Aurelia, Mimi, Rodica and many others gave us a helping hand as well. .

With his talent, Brother Ioanid wrote many poems for children. Their lyrics were very funny:

> *Hop, hop, hop*
> *Goes the little sparrow,*
> *But she knows it's not safe*
>
> *To stay too much on the ground.*
> *So she grabs the grain*
> *And flies up quickly in the sky!*
> *Do the same and fly towards the sky!*

Who would not want to sing songs like:

> *If I had a guitar in my hand,*
> *Zum, zum,*
> *I'd sing from dawn to dusk*
> *Zum, zum,*

Who would you sing to?
To Jesus, Jesus, Jesus!
  Zum, zum, zum zum, zum zum.

Or,

  'What a beautiful phone I have,
  a gift of Jesus:
  My two hands and my thoughts
  that I lift up to heaven!'

The poems were so beautiful and stayed in my mind and heart forever. The children we were ministering to were like our own, and we enjoyed watching them grow. After a number of years many of them weren't children anymore; they had become examples for others, and they started teaching the little ones. . .

It was so satisfying to see those beautiful results in children's ministry. Their beautiful, expressive eyes were engraved in my memory.

Amnesty

One day we learned with great joy that the authorities had issued an amnesty for political prisoners. We were all anxious to see how many of our brothers and sisters would be set free. Sister Binția had told us there were many believers in prison: Brother Richard (her husband), Nicolae Moldoveanu, Traian Dorz, Viski Francis, Vasili Moisescu, Tudose Constantine, Ioan Valer, Alice Panaiodor and many others—all convicted and sentenced to many years because they loved God and did not surrender to the communist beast.

One after the other they were released, fulfilling the words of Psalm 126:

When the LORD turned again the captivity of Zion, we were like them that dream. Then was our mouth filled with laughter, and our tongue with singing: then said they among the heathen, "The LORD hath done great things for them. The LORD hath done great things for us; whereof we are glad."

It was the end of winter 1964, probably in February. I was on maternity leave and kept myself busy with household chores. Vasile was fixing a folding table in our small hallway so we could eat there. Suddenly the door opened slowly and father appeared in the doorway. Before he'd gone to prison I used to call him "Daddy," though he was a tall, solid man. After the years spent in the labor camp he was no longer solid. He had come home. How many nights had I wondered if he would be among the released prisoners? Now there he was in the doorway, shy and skinny, with a bag beside him.

Richard Wurmbrand   Nicolae Moldoveanu   Traian Dorz

Francisc Viski   Vasile Moisescu   Constantin Tudose

Irinca Valer   Alice Panaiodor

It was really him—my daddy, to whom I owed both my biological and my spiritual life. He had led me to my heavenly Father. We rushed and kissed him; then he said, "We ought to thank God first, and then I'd like to take a bath. I'm coming straight from prison and I don't know what I might carry with me. I'm afraid I'm not very clean. That's why I came to you first."

I prepared a hot bath, the way I knew he liked it. What a blessing to have a bathroom! Even now, after such a long time, I can't help but smile when I remember how useful that bathtub was for our friends and guests coming from the provinces, and how many secret baptisms were performed in our bathroom.

My dad, Anghelache

After a while, clean and freshly shaved, my father came out of the bathroom. Meanwhile I called mom and asked her over. Their reunion brought many tears of joy.

That evening my father told us one of the most extraordinary stories I had ever heard.

"Yesterday afternoon the guard opened my cell door and told me I was free to go home. After the formalities were done, I went through the prison gate along with two younger men. As you know, the labor camp was in the middle of the field, far from any village, far from the railroad. Once we got out, we prisoners discussed whether it was better to stay there until morning or try to get to the train station. Snow covered everything. It was windy and cold, and it was going to get dark pretty soon. I had been arrested in the summer and my clothes could not keep me warm in the blizzard. We decided to leave that evening together. Along the way the other two, being younger, went ahead, and after a while I lost sight of them.

"I was alone and tired. The frost was biting fiercely and I was too weak to keep on walking, so I fell down in the snow. I tried to get up a few times until I could not stand up anymore and my legs started getting numb. The cold was slowly seizing my entire body and I realized I would die there, frozen in the snow. I still had the power to pray. "Lord Jesus, please help me get to see my family after all these years of prison."

"I just called out the name of the Lord: 'Jesus! Jesus! Jesus!'" After I whispered His Name I started getting warmer and the heat went slowly upwards, filling my heart as well. I suddenly jumped to my feet and started running with long strides, faster than any human could run. Sometimes my legs would get in front of my body as if driven by something or someone else. I covered that distance so fast that I found myself at the train station in no time.

"I had witnessed a miracle and I was the first one to be amazed by what had happened. It was just like in the story of Apostle Philip who caught up with the eunuch's carriage in the wilderness. Yes, our Lord is the God of miracles."

Dorinel

After we found out I was expecting we prayed continually for the tiny being I was going to deliver. We wanted our baby to enjoy the blessings of heaven and earth, but more than anything to be a child of God, and to have his name written in the Book of Life.

One day when I was praying, the Lord spoke to me in my heart and told me that I would have a boy who would be a believer. That confirmation brought such comfort and joy to me that it was mirrored on my face. Sometimes people would ask me, "What do you want to have, a girl or a boy?" I used to answer, "It doesn't matter what I want because I will have a boy, and he will be faithful to God." People would smile—how could anyone know what the child would be in that time when there were no ultrasounds?

My husband's parents, Eugenia and Vasile, came to visit us all the way from Bucovina. My mother-in-law said to me, "My experience tells me this will be a baby girl."

My father-in-law said to her, somewhat jokingly, "I think she will have a boy and I'm ready to make a bet with you."

I do not remember what the bet was, but they bet on it. I knew who would win, but I let them convince themselves.

The due date was around April 10. On the last Sunday of March when we went to church, I was curious to see if I could still ride a bicycle. I could, but soon after that I had to go to the hospital to deliver the baby. And so our first child was born—a beautiful baby boy—on March 31, 1964. I named him Dorian, because we considered him a gift from God, a perfect gift for us. But in choosing his name we also thought of Aunt Dora's goodness to us.

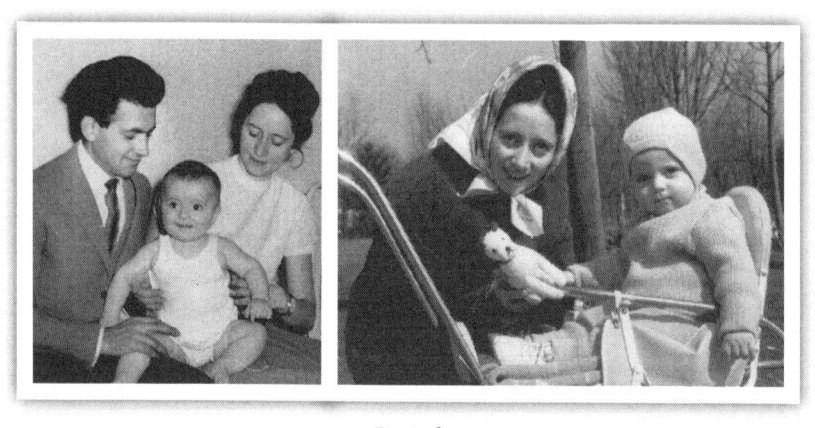

Dorinel

Aunt Alice

When Dorian was born Aunt Alice Panaiodor had just been released from prison. Like many others, she had been sentenced to jail for her faith in God, and had been terribly mistreated there. When she was being interrogated, the Secret Police agents beat her head against the table until they broke her teeth. But she had remained steadfast in her faith. She was a true hero, like Sister Binția, Iuliana Viski and many more. Aunt Alice, as we called her, kept count of her months and years of freedom by thinking of Dorinel's age. He was born the same day she came out of prison. A love bond was created between them and she used to visit us every week. She had no family and we became like her own children.

The release of these prisoners seemed to indicate a certain tolerance of the Communist Party toward believers. We didn't hear of many arrests and persecutions anymore.

Our human nature tends to quickly forget what is unpleasant and to set new dreams that are sometimes too bold.

Alice Panaiodor and Dorinel

Churches were packed. Believers grew considerably in number. Despair and the lack of joy in life drove people to seek God. There's no doubt that true peace, joy and support come only from God. In the midst of those dire circumstances we, as Christians, were living witnesses. We were quite a sight to unbelievers. Though we went through the same hardships, trials and pains of life as other people, we never lost our confidence in God, or the smiles on our faces. We had hope in the One who could lift us up in our times of hardship and who was always by our side. This hope is called faith, and only by faith may we see our hopes fulfilled.

Dorinel's Illness

In the summer of 1964, Dorinel was about 5 or 6 months old. One day he started coughing and he had high fever. Since he was so small, and our first baby, we didn't know what to do. His sickness found us completely unprepared. The fever did not go down the following day either, so I called the doctor. She examined him and told us flatly that he had viral pneumonia and recommended that we hospitalize him. .

He was wheezing whenever he tried to breathe. We went straight to the Pediatric Hospital. Parents were allowed to stay overnight with their children in the hospital only in severe cases, or if they bribed the medical staff. I did everything I could in order to be able to stay with my son in the hospital. Most hospital rooms were large and contained many beds. I was put in a smaller room designed for only two children and their mothers.

I would not have allowed the system to make me leave my baby alone in the hospital. I watched every breath he took, and my heart stopped every time I saw him choking, because he didn't know how to cough and clear his throat. He was under antibiotic treatment but I didn't see any improvement. .

I was trying to pray, and I did pray, but the fear that gripped my heart made me feel my prayer was powerless. I knew I was not supposed to lose heart, because the Lord had promised He would give me a boy who would grow to be His servant. So there was no way I could lose him right then. He had to grow up and get to have a lifetime of serving the Lord.

Though my prayer was weak, my faith wasn't. One Thursday night when I knew my fellow believers would be in church, I asked the other mom to watch my baby too, and I hurried over there.

Congregation at Miulești

The church building was full, as usual. I asked the brother leading the prayer service to pray with the whole congregation for Dorinel. It was a fervent prayer, and many brothers and sisters cried out to God with tears in their eyes. Tears streamed down my face, too. Suddenly a heavenly peace came over me and the fear in my heart was replaced with words of thanks and praise.

After the service I rushed back to the hospital, anxious to see my baby. He was asleep. I asked the mother who had stayed there, "How was he?"

"Oh, he felt really bad; I was about to call the doctor, but around eight o'clock he calmed down and fell asleep."

That was the precise hour when the whole congregation had prayed for him. I knew my son had been healed. "The effective, fervent prayer of a righteous man avails much" (James 5:16).

Dorinel slept well all through the night. The next day, because he no longer had fever and wasn't coughing anymore, the doctor stopped his medication, and after one more day I was able to take him back home. My trust in our living, good, powerful God was strengthened by this experience.

Glimpses of Vasile's Childhood

"Our home became a real Bethany. In the Bible, that was the place where our Lord Jesus used to find His rest. Vasile and I were always glad whenever our brothers and sisters visited us. We were young and eager to be useful for the heavenly kingdom we were part of. We tried to follow the example of the early believers recorded in the book of Acts: they used to gather together from house to house, to help and encourage each other. We also had the living example of Vasile's childhood stories, which I loved listening to.

"My father was very involved in the ministry and he was often away," he told me. "That meant he was going from village to village to speak to people about salvation, to teach believers the true way to heaven and to encourage them in the faith. At home, mother was in charge of the entire household, and she had to care for all the children. Our house hosted frequent gatherings, so I often woke up surrounded by prayer. On one such occasion my father, who had the gift of prophecy, heard himself stating that the Soviets would come and that the wealthy would become penniless.

"After that prayer he asked my mother, "Ghene, what are the Soviets?"

"Much later, after the war, when the Russians invaded our country, they found out who the Soviets were and how they truly impoverished all the people. The wealthy citizens lost all their possessions or ended up in prison."

Sometimes Vasile would tell me stories about his exploits.

"In the summertime there was a lot of work to do, so when Mom had to go somewhere I was in charge of the household. We used those opportunities to play to our hearts' desires. All my friends in the neighborhood would come over and we explored everything and climbed everywhere, even on the rooftop. When we got tired after so much playing we went inside and started baking cakes with the flour mom saved for the holidays. I didn't forget to do the chores that she entrusted to me, but we also had great fun playing. When mother returned, the villagers told her, 'Your boy gathered all the village kids in your yard.'

"I knew what to expect that night. Mom would call me, 'Vasile, get in here right now!' and then I was punished.

"My mom Eugenia, or Ghenea as she was called, was busy from dawn to dusk. One moment she was in the kitchen, the next in the stable or in the garden; with the children; at a prayer meeting; visiting other sisters; or giving advice and help to the needy. And I was her main helper. Early in the morning, when I was still sound asleep, she used to wake me up saying, 'Vasilică, get up!' or 'Vasilică, go fetch water from the well!' 'Vasilică, that horse might have starved to death in the barn!' 'Vasilică, go feed the animals!' 'Take the cows to the pasture!' or 'Come on, hurry up to school!'

"I liked school very much. On the way to school we formed a larger and larger group, to which were added the kids from each house we passed by. At school everything was fine until it was time for Religion class. Our teacher Mr. Cornea was the village priest. He was angry with us, the born-again believers, who had made him lose his parishioners. Since my father was the pastor of our church, I had to pay for it. We began the Religion class with the Lord's Prayer, but I did not make the sign of the cross when we finished it. I was severely and repeatedly beaten for that; the priest would hit the palms of my hands with a stick until they swelled. And yet I loved school, especially History and Geography.

"Sometimes in the evening, I went fishing with one or two more boys from the village. I went to the creek with a torch in my hand. We would watch intently, trying to spot the fish that were sleeping among the stones. I could see them in the light of the torch and pierce them with a fork. They were small, but Mother was very happy to fry them. We used to eat them with garlic sauce and polenta."

Though our childhoods had been very different, they had shaped our character and helped us accept the hardships and use them for our

Holiday

best. However, we tried to offer our own child an easier life and a happier childhood. This way we had the chance to relive ours. We would play in the park in summer or go sleighing in the snow in wintertime. We used to spend the holidays going on different trips together.

The Ioanids and Dorinel at Borsec

One summer when Dorinel was about four years old we went to Borsec with the Ioanids—Sister Leana and Brother Costel. Such a long trip wasn't easy on a train with a small child. We decided to

With the Ioanids at Borsec

take the night train, hoping that Dorinel would sleep most of the trip. When it was time for bed we put him between us and began to tell him a story. It was the story we used to tell him almost every night, The Goat with Three Kids. You know, of course, that the goat told the kids they were allowed to open the door only when they heard her singing a certain song.

When we got to that song the four of us started singing it loudly at first, then we repeated the same chorus more softly until we thought Dorinel had finally fallen asleep, so we could close our eyes and rest as well. But when everything got quiet he would open his tired eyes and ask, "And what did the goat say?"

So we had to start singing the song all over again, loudly at first, then slower and slower. Those were sweet memories with my loved ones . . .

The Wurmbrands Leave Romania

After some foreign intervention, which we knew nothing about, Brother Wurmbrand's family received permission to leave the country.

As for the rest of the population, we were well guarded. The whole army, the Secret Police, and the mined borders with barbed wire protected us from the danger of capitalism. We were told that people there were exploited by a handful of rich people so that they could barely get by. However, I often heard about Romanians who wanted to go to that part of the world, and some who even tried to cross the borders illegally. If life under Communism was so much better compared to life in the capitalist world, how come none of the occidentals tried to escape their own countries to come over to us?

Goodbye meal with the Wurmbrands

The Wurmbrands were going to move to Norway. They belonged to the Church of Norway, and thanks to various interventions they were finally being allowed to leave after years of imprisonment and suffering.

One evening before their departure we were paying a visit to the Wurmbrands when Brother Richard said to us, "You see, my children, with God's help we will go into the free world. Once we get there we'll try to do something for the suffering believers in Romania. We will not be like those who want to spend the rest of their lives with no worries, in luxury and amusement, forgetting where they came from. Absolutely not. We don't know what we will be able to do, but we will try to do our best to give a helping hand. So many brothers who return home from prison don't have enough food to eat. They have no rights or benefits. Many have different health issues. We'll try to send them help, but we need some trustworthy, wise people to work with here, in Romania, to receive the aid and distribute it with the fear of the Lord. It will be a risky activity. We have thought of you. Would you like to work together with us?"

Brother Richard, Dorinel and I

Since becoming a Christian I had prayed for years to be a useful tool in the Kingdom of God, one way or another, and Vasile shared my desire. Many believers thought that the Kingdom would begin only after death, when they got to heaven. As for us, we believed the Kingdom began right here, and if we were not part of it on earth how could we be in heaven? The Lord's Prayer says "Thy Kingdom come, Thy will be done on earth as it is in heaven." And we wanted to do God's will starting from His kingdom here on earth.

Now both of us faced that question. Vasile looked at me and I saw in his eyes the burning desire to serve the Lord. My heart shared the same desire. It was enough to exchange one look, and we knew what we had to do. Our hearts were united toward the fulfillment of the same purpose, so we accepted the offer.

We had no idea what was going to happen after that, and we were not prepared for events that were coming. We had no knowledge about that. We had not eaten of the tree of knowledge of good and evil, like Adam and Eve. We had tasted only of the tree of life and love for our Lord, and we were happy with Him.

> *In the years of your youth,*
> *When you're full of zeal, like the psalmist,*
> *It is so good to give to Christ*
>
> *All your longings and all your years!*
> *—In the Years of Your Youth, by C. Ioanid*

In the evenings that followed we discussed the ways everything we'd talked about could be achieved. We had heard about the names of some Christians who had returned from prison. Most were part of denominations we had almost no contact with. But who had not heard of brothers like Niculiță Moldoveanu, Traian Dorz, or the Viski family whom I had had the privilege to meet personally? After all, suffering did not select people according to religious principles, and religion had not helped anyone in their times of trouble. Only faith and love in Jesus had value, and all these people were genuine witnesses of the faith they had proven by their steadfastness in the midst of torture.

Sister Anuța

In late spring, the lime trees scented the air in Bucharest, especially in our neighborhood. The evening breeze carried the intoxicating fragrance through all the open windows.

We liked to take walks with Dorinel in the evening. We were getting to know each other better and talked often about our past experiences, about how we felt, and about our future aspirations. Sometimes, however, we just walked in silence. It's interesting how two people who love each other have a sense of fulfillment and confidence just by being in the presence of one another, and they don't need any words. The look in their eyes reveals their heart condition. Those days when we were both busy with our jobs we could hardly wait to get back home to be together again. Though no life of ease or amusement was waiting for us there—just all the housework—we were together. We did not expect declarations of love, but we knew our relationship was impregnated with love. We were trying to please each other in all the little things we did every day: a favorite food, a kind word, a smile. On the 7th day of every month, the day of our marriage, Vasile used to buy me flowers. I loved the flowers, but I was even more impressed that my husband loved to remember that day.

On one of those late spring evenings someone knocked on our door. It was a Romanian sister from Norway, Anuța Moise, who was "visiting" the country. She had left Romania many years ago and was the first messenger sent by our Brother Richard. Our hearts started beating really fast. It was the first visit of someone coming from the free world, a world in which people could travel anywhere they wanted.

How excited we were! So, we had not been forgotten. The plan we had talked about was still on, and we were ready to get the work started. Or so we thought.

Sister Anuța brought us news of the Wurmbrand family, but also clothes and money for the families we were supposed to take care of. She also told us that someone would come soon with a clandestine shipment of Bibles for us to distribute secretly.

We knew how the Communist regime hated and tried to confiscate Bibles. They loathed this book. They said there was no God, so they could afford to commit all kinds of atrocities. But the Bible says that God exists, He's alive, and He's good and forgiving. It also says there will be a Judgment Day when all people will be held accountable for their deeds. The Bible and the Christians were in full opposition to the communist ideology. Communists could have full control over all people by means of intimidation, but they could not make the Christians submit to them, because the latter were obeying God more than any human form of authority. So we were fully aware we had to be very careful not to put anyone in danger through our underground ministry.

We became very fond of Sister Anuţa; we loved her stories about the free world she was now living in. The things she told us seemed taken out of storybooks. What a pleasure to listen to. We could hardly believe that the women in Norway and other free countries put their dirty dishes in a box and then took them out of there perfectly clean. I wished I could have a chance to see such a miracle.

Dorinel had decided to "marry" Sister Anuţa when he got older, and she agreed to wait for him, though she was almost 60. It seems she kept her part of the deal, because she never got married.

Soon it was time for her to leave. She told us an American brother would come soon to bring the Bibles, and we also talked about the possibility of getting a car to use in order to fulfill our mission.

In Romania at that time, one could only buy a Dacia, the only car made in our country, and for that one had to save money for years and then wait some more years until it was their turn to receive the car. We could not even have such high hopes. The only solution would have been to get a car as a gift from some "relatives" or friends in the West.

Sister Anuţa returned to Norway with all that information and we were left thinking more of the car ... and less of the risks we were taking. That's how youth is!

Were we going to get a VW Bug? Those cars were small, but at least they had four wheels and the rain couldn't come inside.

The idea of having a car of our own seemed like a dream, especially to Vasile, who already had some driving experience. He signed up for driving classes because he wanted to get his driving license by the time the car would arrive. And then we waited and waited and waited. We also started to learn a little bit of English.

~PART SIX~
Smuggling and Singing

Bill and Brian

The wait seemed long, but one evening we got some unexpected company: two American couples, Bill and Henriette Bathman, and Brian and Gwen Bounds, with their little girl Wendy.

We were always happy to receive guests, and were used to having a full house. The Lord had always multiplied our food and cakes for them, but this time was different. Our guests were coming from the free world, the world of Sister Anuța, and they spoke another language. They were speaking English while we were using mostly sign language. However, the Spirit of the Lord helped us understand each other.

Bill and Brian

Brian and Gwen sang beautifully together and Bill could whistle as sweet as a lark. Little Wendy was very cute, so it didn't take long for Dorinel to realize how lovely she was. In a few minutes they were already good friends, so they spread their toys on the floor and started playing together.

The Action Plan

Our guests won our hearts and we received them with brotherly love.

The purpose of their visit was to get to know us and make plans together for the work that lay before us. During their next visit one of them, was supposed to bring a car, that we were going to register in Vasile's name, as a gift from abroad. Then they were going to bring Bibles to Romania with their own car.

These were the steps of their plan:

- The Bibles were going to be hidden in the secret compartments of their car that had been built precisely for the purpose of not being discovered when crossing the border.
- Our name and address, as well as the route to our place were only memorized—not written down anywhere. They had to be very cautious so that nobody could identify us as their contact in Romania. Our foreign brothers had even memorized the number of steps they had to climb to our apartment.
- The Bibles could not be brought to our home. The contact persons had to keep them in the hidden compartments of their car, leave the car somewhere on a street, and then come to our house as if they were taking a walk, after making sure they were not followed. When we met, we established a meeting place for later. Afterward they would take the Bibles out of the hiding place and put them in bags.

The following part of the plan was our responsibility and we fulfilled it for over 10 years. We usually worked like this:

- At a certain hour in the evening our contacts were waiting in their car on a street in our neighborhood, which we had decided at our previous meeting.
- We would drive our car and slowly past theirs, making sure they recognized us, then they followed us to the place where the Bibles were going to be moved from their car to ours.
- After that they left right away, so nobody would notice our contact

with a car that had a foreign license plate.

Our partners' mission ended there, while ours was just beginning. We could not keep the Bibles in our apartment. It was too small, too central, and too many people passed by. Our neighbors could watch all our activities through the window.

Vasile had to find trustworthy people who lived further away from the city and who had the courage to store larger quantities of Bibles. He was to take the books from them in smaller quantities and distribute them later where they were greatly needed.

This was the general plan. Now it remained to see how we were going to apply it. Who were we supposed to work with, and whom could we trust? Where could we find storage places? Who would we distribute the Bibles to? We needed answers for all these questions.

The Secret Police informers and agents were everywhere. We could never be sure what kind of people we were talking to. The Secret Police had their own ways of making people fear them. They used to approach someone using a method they tried on us as well. It went like this: "You are an intelligent person. If you cooperate with us you will prove your loyalty to the country. All you need to do is be vigilant and notice anything out of the ordinary, or any unusual activity of other citizens and report it to us. Then your job will be secured." (In this way they suggested to the person they approached that he could lose his job in case he didn't want to cooperate.) "We know everything that's going on, and we want to see your devotion to the motherland."

Out of fear, people turned into informers. Some would even spy on their own family members, neighbors in their apartment building, coworkers, members of their church, and people on the street. The country was full of informers. They would even spy on one another. We could never know if a person we interacted with was an informer or not, unless the Spirit of God revealed it to us, or if that person gave himself away.

Bibles were tracked, seized and destroyed by the Communists. But people who loved and feared God could not truly agree with the Communist doctrine. Believers knew they had to live in such a way that they would do the will of the One who died on the cross for them, and by whom they were going to be held accountable one day.

So, after much prayer and thought, Vasile started to prepare the first transfer. We were excited, and did not fully realize the danger to which we were really exposing ourselves.

Our First Car

As he had promised, Bill returned soon with a car for us. It was on older model Opel Record, but it still worked very well.

This was the beginning of a whole new experience for us. Once we

Opel Record, our first car

received the car we got involved in a series of new activities that could not possibly go unnoticed. Because Vasile used the car for his daily activities as well, it would not be obvious when he drove it to take Bibles from one place to another.

That car was also a blessing for other brothers who went to preach the gospel or take the elements of the Lord's Supper to nearby villages. Countless times my husband was able to take Brother Vasile Șandor and Costică Caraman to many different village churches.

I'll mention just a few of these trips.

- At Vizureşti, a village situated near Bucharest, a baptism service had to be performed secretly. Brother Şandor asked Vasile if he could take him there. They drove to Vizureşti, arriving in the evening. Parking the car on a hill at the entrance to the village, they walked to a house where several believers had gathered together. Among them were those who had asked to be baptized. In those days only the believers' children could be baptized. Water baptism was forbidden for anyone else, so adult baptisms were done in secret for all those who received the faith.

Vasile and Dida Şandor

The ministers preached, explaining the importance of baptism, and the congregation sang and prayed. When it got dark outside, baptismal candidates put on white shirts, left through the back door, and walked to a creek. In the moonlight, those dressed in white looked like angels.

Late that night after Brother Şandor finished the baptisms they returned to our car. Several brothers pushed it downhill to avoid the noise of turning on the engine. When they got to the bottom of that slope, Vasile would get the car started and off they went.

Another time Brother Caraman asked my husband to go with him to a gypsy village, because some people there had opened their hearts to the Lord. The village was near Bucharest. Gypsies there were utterly bad. Everyone was afraid of them, especially of the big bullies and slashers. The area inhabited by gypsies was at the periphery of the village and the houses there had no fences. Some gypsies who were in the street at the time of our arrival came toward us. Our car made them curious. They kept following our car to see where we were going, all the more so as we drove very slowly because of the rough and dusty road. A large crowd of men, women and children came after us, disregarding the dust stirred up on the road.

We stopped at the house of the man who wanted to follow Jesus, to whom Brother Caraman had spoken. The crowd also stopped there, waiting to see what would happen. In their village they seldom had a chance to see someone driving a car. Brother Caraman started speaking to them about salvation and faith in Jesus.

Brother Constantin Caraman

We told them that we all sin, some more than others, and explained that the differences were not so important. We showed that the punishment for our sins is hell, but that we have a chance to be saved by believing that Jesus is the Son of God and that He took our place on the cross. If He becomes our Savior and Lord, we are no longer punished, but God the Father receives us and makes us His children. In the end, the preacher asked, "Is there anyone here who wants to receive Lord Jesus by faith?"

Many of them had tears in their eyes. All hands were raised.

"Put your hands down," said Brother Caraman. "You don't understand. When you receive Jesus by faith, you no longer go out stealing. You don't live with another man's wife. Your life must be changed. Only those who want to receive this faith should raise their hand."

And again, all hands were raised.

"You still didn't get it, said the preacher. Put your hands down.

When you receive Christ by faith you don't lie anymore, you don't swear, you don't fight, but you start a brand new life. Take your time and think about your decision. Now raise your hand only if you really understood what this is about."

All hands were raised again. It was we who did not understand that the Spirit of the Lord had touched their hearts.

After the service some women came to ask me, weeping, "Is there forgiveness for me as well? I had several abortions. Do you think God can really forgive me?" Others said, "I've taken another woman's husband. Can God forgive me?"

The example of the thief who was crucified next to the Savior helped them understand that the sacrifice and the blood of Jesus forgave any sin.

After some time, a gypsy congregation was founded in that village. The number of robberies and fights decreased. The biggest bully in the village repented and became a good example for many.

One would have thought that the authorities would be glad to witness such a change, but they were not. They began to persecute the new believers, trying to stop them from gathering together and praying, as well as from sharing their faith. On one such occasion, the former bully told them, "If you don't leave us alone, I'll show you what I'm capable of. I'll set my new faith aside for a few minutes and I'll scare you to death."

The threat seemed to work, at least for a while . . .

We often gave Brother Niculiță Moldoveanu a ride to different prayer gatherings in the nearby villages.

- Sometimes we organized secret meetings with Brother Traian Dorz (who was under house arrest).
- We met in meadows and forests where we talked and sang together. Brother Niculiță brought his accordion and we would sing together in the woods. Then we took them all home before returning to our apartment.

- Sometimes we would meet Brother Costache Ioanid and Brother Aurel Popescu.

With the Moldoveanu family in Săsciori

In the woods with Brother Traian

God's Faithfulness in Communist Romania   103

Aurel and Valerica Popescu, Nicolae Moldoveanu, Vasile and I

Brother Costache Ioanid and Nicolae Moldoveanu

In the forest with Brother Moldoveanu

First Bible Shipment

It is said that when you wait for the arrival of your first child you prepare carefully; nevertheless, when labor begins you still panic. Something similar happened to us. We had done our best to be prepared for the ministry that was awaiting us, but we still felt we were not ready. We were excited to know that we had such a treasure as the Bible. Since Romania was under a Communist regime, the Scripture was not printed in our country, neither was it for sale, and the authorities were tracking down Bibles wherever they could.

Romania was an Orthodox country and in the Orthodox Church only the priest had a Bible. Once the Evangelical movement entered our country, every believer was expected to read the Scriptures for himself; so the need for Bibles increased enormously. The Pentecostal movement had appeared in Romania only shortly before Communism. Then suffering and the lack of freedom brought faith in God closer to the people's hearts. Romanians were very open to receive God and His message in the Bible. The Holy Book was not easily available in those days, but we received a significant amount.

Our excitement was understandable, considering the treasure in our possession. And our treasure was stored under the hay in Papa Man's barn. He lived on the edge of the city. A dirt road went from the tram station to his house. In summer, we could get there by car, wagon or on foot. When the weather was rainy or snowy and the road got muddy, it was very hard to get there. The two kilometers to his house seemed like twenty with our loaded suitcases. However, we carried them with such joy! That's where we kept our treasure, well guarded by Papa Man. He was the father-in-law of Vasile's sister Viorica.

Vasile got Bibles from him only when a need arose. With the car Bill gave us we

Brother Aurel Man

traveled all over the country. We used to put one or two layers of Bibles, one layer of clothes, then some blankets on top of them, and that's how we improvised a bed for Dorinel. We told those who wanted to know that we were going on a family trip. Sometimes the car looked like a heavy duck under the weight inside, though Dorinel was as light as a feather.

Carwash

Given the rough roads we had to travel, from time to time we had to stop by a creek and wash the dust and mud off of our car.

Wheel Exchange

The bumpy roads in Romania made our tires wear out quickly. Vasile took as good care of them as possible, but sooner or later he had to replace them and that was very complicated. In Romanian stores at that time we could not find any tires for Opels. Bill promised he would bring us some from Germany. However, when he crossed the border it would not be easy to explain why he had five spare tires for a regular tourist trip. That would have aroused the suspicion of the customs officers.

Then Bill came up with a great idea. He went to Germany with a car similar to ours and bought some new tires for it. He drove all the way to Bucharest, and at nightfall he met Vasile on a side street to exchange wheels. They parked the cars one behind the other. Both men removed the wheels of their cars and then exchanged them, working as fast as they could, hoping they would not be noticed.

When they parted, Vasile had four new tires and a spare wheel, while Bill's were extremely worn.

Bill prayed all the way back that he would be able to get safely to Germany with those tires. He was amused, seeing the bewilderment on the faces of the mechanics who had just put the new tires on his car a few days ago.

"Sir, what happened to your tires?" they asked him.

"The roads I've been driving on were terrible," replied Bill laughing.

Christmas Celebration

Our family life now had a new meaning. Though we had no time to waste and were always busy, our life was worth living. Vasile was increasingly involved in the work of Bible distribution, and he was gone most of the day. I was just as busy. In the morning I had to go to the lab. In order to get there I took the trolley from the corner of our street to Kogălniceanu. I got off there and took a bus to the North Train Station. Crossing that square I took one more bus to the Geological Institute. I worked eight hours a day, returning in the evening by the same means of transportation. Sometimes I had to stop and stand in line to buy some food. Once I got home I had to cook the meal, take care of our son, do the laundry and all the other housework. In our congregation I was still involved as a Sunday school teacher for the kids and teenagers who wanted to learn more from the Bible, and to sing and recite poems in our church. I was so fond of them all!

One winter when we were getting ready for the Christmas celebration, the children had learned one of Brother Ioanid's poems, One Star Has Fallen, and several of them were reciting the lines of the different characters. Some were the lambs, one boy was the storyteller, and another one was the donkey who said, with the poet's well known sense of humor:

> And then the donkey wearing the saddle
> Said as if reading from a book:
> "There are many things in this world,
> But in order to know them all
> You must have traveled far and wide!
> And not everybody's a donkey like me."

For the Christmas Eve celebration in our church we used to prepare one small bag of sweets for each child. It was a difficult job, since we had lots of children but limited resources. We had to count every single item to make sure we had enough for everybody. Brother Macovei, one of the elders in our congregation, used to count all the children (and add a few more bags for the potential visitors), from the newborn to the 14–15 year olds.

After standing in lines for hours to buy the sweets, we were able to put in the bags one orange, some apples, chocolates, biscuits and candies. All the bags had to have the same content. The youth group helped us pack everything.

The hundreds of little bags made a big pile. The afternoon before the evening service we would put them all in the car and take them to church, where Brother Macovei would keep a close eye on them, making sure no "mouse" would sneak in to grab something. We could not risk losing any of them. After the children's program we used to give them the gifts.

I still remember with regret one Christmas Eve when we were distributing the bags and Brother Macovei, who was assisting me, said. "Sister, save one bag for me too."

I thought he was joking. He knew all the bags were counted. I smiled, thinking he didn't really mean it. When the pile of bags was getting smaller and smaller he reminded me:

"Don't forget to save one for me."

I still didn't take him seriously and kept on distributing the bags until there was not a single one left. With moist eyes Brother Macovei asked me: "How come you didn't keep a bag for me, sister?"

I felt like crying when I saw he had been serious all along, and I realized how much he would have wanted a handful of those sweets he had guarded all day long.

"Brother Macovei, I thought you were joking. Please forgive me. Here, please take my son's bag."

"No sister, if you haven't kept one for me, I do not need somebody else's bag."

In that Communist paradise, not only the children were eager to have some sweets.

We could only find bananas and oranges in the food stores before Christmas. They were expensive, and most people could not afford to buy them. Even so, one had to be lucky to be near the store when the fruits were brought in, and then stand in line to buy some before they would run out of stock.

Christmas Carols

After the Christmas Eve service we used to go caroling. Though the Nativity of the Lord Jesus had received the new name of "Winter Holidays" and Santa Claus had been replaced with Jack Frost, caroling was not prohibited. Children went caroling from door to door, in buses or trams, and got a few pennies. With a group of believers we used to sing songs that praised the birth of our Lord. It was Vasile and I, Valerica and Aurel Popescu, Leana and Costel Ioanid, as well as others who wanted to join us. Sister Valerica had a beautiful voice. We usually visited those who could not come to church, because we knew they would be happy to have us. I would not for the world have given up the opportunity of singing on the streets about the love and birth of our Savior.

I remember one Christmas Eve. It was past midnight when we arrived at Sister Olguța and Brother Franco's (we used to call him Hombre). We started singing Silent Night and the carol sounded like an angelic choir had descended from heaven, breaking the silence of the night. Sister Olguța woke up and did not dare to open her eyes. She believed she was dreaming and didn't want to wake up for fear it would all go away. But we were standing at her door, so she got up and let us in where we sang one more carol, Oh, What Wonderful News!

Brother Costel and Sister Leana Ioanid, part of our group, were tired and frozen. At some point we lost sight of them. They had gone home because they lived in the neighborhood. A little later we went home too, because next morning we had a regular work day ahead of us. But the fatigue did not matter. We were young and we had the chance to go caroling only once a year, on Christmas Eve.

Dick the Dutchman

The Bible and aid shipments were becoming more and more frequent. Missionaries communicated between them, and our name and address were written down in their notebooks. We had started our underground work with Sister Anuța, and with Bill and Brian, but after that, on many other occasions we did not even ask the missionaries their names. It was better not to know them or the organization they represented. There were several organizations and all had the same goal: to bring Bibles and religious literature, and food and clothing for the needy, especially for the persecuted believers.

We worked with many missionaries and never took this underground activity lightly. Therefore we prayed every time and asked the Lord's protection over us and them alike. We worked in spite of fear, especially me, but the love for the Lord surpassed the fear of men. If we fell into the hands of men we knew that God was there to deliver us, but who could have saved us from the hand of God if we dishonored Him?

Many of the people we worked with we met only once, and they did not return to Romania after that. But we became good friends with those who came more often. One of the latter was Dick Langeveld from the Netherlands. He was part of the "Open Doors" Mission. He was a tall, thin elderly man, a very nice person and also a biologist.

The mission he worked with was very well organized. Any work plan had four phases and involved four groups of people with different but complementary responsibilities:

- The purpose of the first group was to establish a contact.
- The second group dealt with crossing the necessary material over the border.
- The third one had to immediately check and report if everything went well.
- A fourth group, which was the largest and the most important, had to support in prayer the whole operation, asking the Lord's protection over those who were gone on the mission field.

It was hard to understand how they managed to cross the border with such a large number of Bibles, especially when their cars were sometimes searched carefully, piece by piece! Either God blinded the customs officers, or He made the Bibles disappear.

Brother Dick told once about a funny experience of his:

"I had an appreciable amount of Bibles hidden in the secret compartments of my car. In order to create a diversion I got some frogs in a cage and put them in the car. Through a friend I was able to get a document issued by the Dutch Biological Institute stating that those frogs were part of an experiment. Of course that "document" had no value, but it had the header of the Dutch Biological Institute printed on it and it was addressed to the Biological Institute in Bucharest. The frogs were supposed to be used for a "scientific study".

"I put the cage with the frogs next to me on the front seat of the car. At the border I waited for my turn to be checked by the customs officers. When they saw the cage with frogs, they were shocked at first and then they burst into laughter."

"Sir, what do you have there in the cage?" they asked me.

"Some lab species," I replied unfazed.

"What lab species? I see only some frogs there."

"Gentlemen, these frogs are part of a scientific study," I continued.

"What kind of study, sir? You are not allowed to bring any frogs into Romania. Take that cage outside so we can inspect it!"

Lots of people had already gathered around us and everyone was laughing.

"Gentlemen, please be very careful. I can't afford to lose any of them."

"Take the frogs out of the cage so we can inspect them!"

"I can't. If I do they will be gone and so will be my study."

"Take the frogs out!" they insisted.

"With feigned indignation and worry I pulled the cage out. And as expected, when the customs officer opened the cage, the frogs jumped out and started bouncing everywhere while I was chasing them, yelling angrily.

"All the people around were laughing. My "desperate" attempts to find my papers from the Institute and get the frogs back were finally successful.

"When the laughing subsided, I took the frogs, they read the "document" and allowed me to leave.

"After driving for a few miles I stopped the car and thanked God that I'd been able to cross the border without having my car inspected. I threw the frogs away."

His story was fun, but the task we had to achieve from there on was neither easy nor simple. However, God was in control over everything.

Our Network

We were close friends with brothers and sisters from all Christian denominations. As long as we shared the fundamental principles of faith we could work together.

We had lots to learn in this area. We got in contact with believers who had proved their faith by suffering for Jesus, having been confined for years in Communist prisons for the sake of their Lord. Who were we then to judge them?

We had a network of people we worked with and a method we used. We limited our network to people we could fully trust and who often thought they were our only coworkers. It was also best for them to keep a low profile.

In each area of the country Vasile found a place to store the Bibles and the other goods received from abroad, and he had only one contact person in each place to get in touch with when he needed to. That believer was in charge of distributing the Bibles his own area. Nobody knew we had something to do with what was going on there. Sometimes we learned of a certain need in an area, but we did not interfere directly. We only mentioned the situation to our local contact person.

If we happened to meet someone we knew when we were traveling, we always told them we were on a family trip. Dorinel accompanied us almost everywhere when we had to take Bibles or other goods somewhere in the country.

Usually, when we had to cover longer distances, Vasile drove at night when there were fewer policemen on the road. The backseats of our car could be turned into a bed, where we used to place the Bibles, cover them with clothes and a blanket, and Dorinel would sleep on top of them.

One night, we were on the way to Sibiu when a policeman stopped us at a checkpoint. He came to our window and asked Vasile:

"Where are you going at this late hour and what's in the car?"

"Shh! Please do not talk so loud! The child is sleeping in the back. We're going on vacation," said Vasile.

The policeman looked inside, saw Dorinel sleeping in the back, and let us go. We didn't wait for him to change his mind.

One day we had a visitor, a sister from California, Nina Denisiu. She had been born in Romania but had left the country long ago. She was a good friend of the Wurmbrands, who had given her our address.

We gave her a tour to see her friends and relatives in Romania and also took her to visit the brothers who had returned from prison. This is how we met Sister Bușilă, a Baptist believer. She played the organ in the Baptist church in Basarab. She lived in the attic of the church building. We became friends with her and she was a great help in our activity. We often stored Bibles in her tiny home. Besides, we could also count on her support in prayer.

Brothers Valer, Moldoveanu and Dorz with Sister Denisiu and the Viskis

"You are young and very busy so you do not have as much time for prayer as I do," she said once. "Therefore, when I cannot sleep at night, I start praying for you."

We cherished this precious sister. She was of Russian origin, and through her we came to meet Lidia, a sister who was visiting her from Chișinău.

Sister Lidia told us about the Russian believers' great need for Bibles and material assistance.

Our sisters in Chișinău had a special women's ministry. They often gathered to copy the Bible, and their manuscripts were then sent to Siberia where no Christian literature whatsoever was allowed. In order to copy the Bible they needed pens and ink, which were hard to find there. On her departure, we did our best to provide Sister Lidia with as many pens as she wanted. She gave us her address in Chișinău, in case anyone would ever be able to get there with some aid and some Bibles.

Sister Denisiu also introduced us to Ana Florea, an Adventist sister.

Her husband had been convicted because of his faith and had died in prison. Brother Richard Wurmbrand, who had been imprisoned with him, told us an impressive experience about this man:

"The believers in our cell decided to have the Lord's Supper. We had no bread, no wine and no table to put the elements on. We decided to substitute these elements with what we had and to consider them real by faith. Brother Florea, a real saint in our midst, was dying. We chose to use his chest as a table for the Lord's Supper."

Sister Ana Florea

Sister Denisiu brought a few goods to help her. Sister Florea helped us store some of the Bibles at her place, because she lived on the outskirts of Bucharest.

Another coworker who helped us store Bibles was Eugen, Sister Denisiu's nephew. He was our age. We became friends and came to trust him, even though he was a party member. He became a useful helper in our network. Vasile had entrusted him with the spare key to our car. According to an understanding between them, Vasile would take our car loaded with Bibles to a particular place; Eugen took it from there, emptied it and brought it back. The two of them did not even meet in the process.

One of our friends was Mr. Cafengiu, a drawing and sculpture teacher. He was part of the Brethren Church on Carol Davila Street, a short distance from our apartment. He offered to help us store Bibles too, and he had an ingenious idea. In one of the rooms of their headquarters (where no one could suspect Bibles were hidden), lived the widow of Brother Tudor Popescu, the pioneer of their movement. He was friends with the Cafengiu family. During a visit, Mr. Cafengiu brought a few bags filled with Bibles, which he deposited in a storage room of the building, among other forgotten things, before he met Mrs. Popescu.

He could not store large amounts of Bibles there, but the hiding place was useful nevertheless, all the more so as it was close to our apartment. It was an ideal place for smaller quantities.

Our underground activity continued successfully due to the prayers of all our brothers and sisters who supported us.

~ PART SEVEN ~
# Crossing Boarders

The Escapade

We longed to be able to cross the border and visit any other foreign country except for the Soviet Union. In those days it was not easy to get a passport. The authorities needed to be sure we would not try to flee the Communist paradise. This is how, together with Sandu Franco (whose nickname was Uncle Hombre), we applied for a trip to Yugoslavia.

After our request was declined several times, one day it was finally approved. Vasile and I could both go, but without our son. He was the guarantee that we would return to Romania. Dorinel was about five years old and he was going to stay with his grandparents.

Uncle Hombre was Jewish, and also a brother in Christ. Short and plump, he would make people smile just by looking at his serious face.

In his youth he had been a Secret Police officer. He had

Sandu Franco and I in Belgrade

worked in prisons and interrogated many prisoners ruthlessly. I do not know the details of his marriage to Olga, a young woman who received Christ in Brother Wurmbrand's congregation. This is how he came to know God's Word and to receive Jesus as his Savior.

Brother Richard was in prison at that time and no one knew anything about him. He was believed to be dead, since he could not be found anywhere. Franco had access to the records of all the prisoners, and by studying the photo and the name he discovered that Brother Richard was listed under another name so that no one would be able to track him. His pseudonym was Georgescu.

Franco revealed that secret to his family, who were able to find him this way and later, to help Brother Richard get out of prison.

Because of this Franco lost his job immediately and was sentenced to prison. After he was released, he dedicated himself to the work of God, and that's when we got to know him. His wife, Olga, was Jewish as well.

Yugoslavia, the country the three of us had received a tourist visa for, was a Communist country, just like ours. President Tito, however, had turned away from the party line established by Moscow and had become the black sheep of the communist bloc. He allowed Yugoslav citizens to visit any other country without restrictions. Because people could travel freely anywhere they wanted, they were not tempted to "flee" from their country.

Belgrade

We took the train to Yugoslavia and got off in Belgrade.

We were not allowed to take money with us, except for a few lei we exchanged at the border, but that amount was way too small. However, we had taken with us some food, so as not to spend too much on our meals, and had brought some cotton clothes, which we hoped we would be able to sell there to get some money.

Stopping in a public market, we spread our "merchandise" on the pavement and managed to sell it. With that money, we wanted to take the train from Belgrade to Maribor, close to the Austrian border, and try to get into Austria and after that to Vienna.

Going into a free country and watching with our own eyes a world we had only imagined was quite a bold idea.

Milly, a missionary friend of ours, lived in Vienna. She was an old lady who had visited us years ago and had told us, "If you ever come to Vienna I'll be glad to host you." She had given us her phone number and address. Now we had the opportunity to go to Vienna, and she was our hope.

We were taking a big risk. If we got caught in Yugoslavia while trying to cross the Austrian border illegally, we could end up in jail without any chance of ever leaving the country again. But we were already halfway, on a Yugoslav train, and we did not need a visa to go to Austria. We just needed the money for the train tickets. The money we had got for our merchandise was not enough for a "vacation" in Austria.

We bought train tickets from Belgrade to Zagreb. In Zagreb we got on the train going to Vienna, but we bought tickets only to Maribor, for otherwise somebody could discover our intention of getting to Austria.

In Maribor, the last train station before the Austrian border, we got off the train, making sure nobody was watching us, and when the train got moving, we jumped back on. We sat inside an empty compartment. We had no train tickets for that part of our trip.

We waited fearfully for the ticket check. Now there was no turning back—the next train station was in Austrian territory. I was looking out the window to see the border, and the patrol that would check the passengers.

The passport control came first, and we had no problem there. When the customs officer wanted to stamp our passports with the Austrian visa we asked him not to do it. Uncle Hombre explained to him in German that we would get into trouble when we returned to Romania if our officers saw that visa. He was an understanding man and didn't stamp our passports.

The ticket control came next and, as I have already mentioned, we didn't have any tickets.

"Your tickets, please."

None of us said one word. All of a sudden we were not speaking any language anymore.

"Your tickets!"

We used sign language to explain to the train conductor that we didn't have tickets, but we offered him some salami instead. The train conductor was pissed off.

"What salami are you talking about? You'll get off at the next stop!"

We nodded in agreement. The next train stop was in Gratz, Austria.

We were in seventh heaven: we were in Austria and we hadn't got caught. We could already see ourselves around Sister Milly's dining table; we were starving.

We got off in Gratz and bought tickets for the next train to Vienna. We were tired, dirty and hungry, but happy. Our adventure was going to end soon.

The train to Vienna was elegant and comfortable. We went to the toilet, where we washed with scented soap and warm water, then we put on some clean clothes and tried to take a nap.

In the huge Vienna train station we got lost seeing all those advertisements and lights we were not used to, and didn't know which way to go.

We found a cab and gave the driver Sister Milly's address, keeping our eyes on the screen that displayed the cost of our ride. The price was increasing with every passing minute, but fortunately the drive was not too long.

When we got to the house, it was getting dark. We had not told Milly about our trip because it was dangerous to call from Romania to someone who lived abroad. All phone calls were listened to by the Secret Police.

We knocked on her door and waited to see the surprised and happy face of our dear friend. After a few moments, the door was opened by a stranger who gave us an unfriendly look. "What do you want?"

"We are looking for a lady called Milly," said Sandu in German. We don't know her last name.

"I don't know anyone by that name. I just moved in here a couple of weeks ago. Ask some other neighbors who have lived here longer."

We knocked on the next door and asked the neighbor if they knew the person who used to live next door, describing Milly. The lady told us she didn't know anyone by that name; however, a lady that matched our description had lived there but had moved recently. Unfortunately, she did not know her new address.

In that moment all our dreams were shattered. We were disappointed and dismayed. It was late, we were hungry and exhausted, and we had only a few coins left. I do not even remember how we got back to the train station. We thought we could spend the night sleeping there on a bench. But there were no benches in the train station, and nobody sat down on the pavement.

I saw a hotel across the street, and although we didn't have enough money, we decided to take a room there for that night.

At the hotel we remembered Brian and Bill. Their missionary organization was based in Austria as well, at Grossmain near Salzburg, but that was far away from Vienna. I had their phone number. Perhaps they knew where Sister Milly had moved. It was worth a try. Uncle Hombre called from the receptionist's phone, since we didn't have one in our room, and a lady answered. It was Henriette, Bill's wife. She said that Bill and Brian were in Africa, and she did not know anyone named Milly.

Before the end of the call she asked us where we were. Sandu told her we were in a hotel next to the train station in Vienna, and he hung up.

We returned silently to our room and ate some canned food. We were sad and thoughtful. Who was to blame?

We were dead tired, but who could have gone to sleep now? Our situation was desperate. I felt like crying, but I thought that would have been embarrassing.

Suddenly, in the silence of the night, someone knocked on the door:

"Mr. Răscol, Mr. Răscol, there's a phone call for you!"

We all jumped up, not knowing what to expect. Nobody knew about our trip to Vienna. Who could it be? Maybe it was a mistake, but still the person on the phone had specifically asked about Vasile.

With Milly in Vienna

Sandu and Vasile went downstairs immediately. I stayed in the room and the few minutes that passed until their return seemed like an eternity. They came back smiling happily and told me all in one breath: "It was Sister Milly. I don't know how she found us, but tomorrow morning she comes here to meet us."

This was hard to believe. We thanked God and went to bed peacefully. The next day, we were happy and talkative. We got ready to meet Milly.

Her coming made all our fears and worries go away. We were eager to know how she had found us. What was the miracle behind our getting together? After we hugged each other warmly she told us, "Let's go eat and I'll tell you the whole story while we have breakfast."

She didn't have to insist. A warm and tasty meal was more than welcome after all the canned food we had eaten lately. While we were having breakfast, Sister Milly told us, "When you talked to Bill's wife last night she realized that you were in a desperate situation. She started to think: 'Who could Milly be?' I didn't use my real name when I was in Romania. My real name is Mildred. Bill's wife thought that I could be the Milly you were looking for, and she called me, asking if I knew a certain Romanian family named Răscol."

"Yes, I've been in their home," I said.

"Well, they are now in Vienna and are looking for you at your old address."

"And where are they now?"

"At a hotel near the train station."

"Which train station? There are several of them, and which hotel? There are dozens around each train station!"

"That's all I know. They are in a hotel near the train station."

"Then I started calling all the hotels around the train stations and I finally found you."

Milly had come by car, and she took us for a ride to see the city. She showed us the President's House, then we went to Prater Amusement

Park. At lunch we had some roast chicken, and then she asked us very seriously: "Children, would you like to stay here? Do you want to apply for political asylum and never go back to Communist Romania?"

Uncle Hombre and Vasile were ready to stay. The opportunity to choose freedom over constraints did not come often in those times, and now we had that amazing opportunity without even looking for it. Many others had risked their lives to get into a free country. But all I could see in my mind was the image of my son. It was true that we had left him in good hands. He was with my parents who adored him, but they were his grandparents, while I was his mother, and I could not abandon my child for the whole world. Nobody could convince me that if we stayed in Austria I would be able to see him again; therefore, no one could convince me to remain abroad. There was no doubt in my heart. A mother cannot leave her baby.

And so, after a couple of wonderful days, with gifts we had bought for our families, the three of us returned home, back behind the Iron Curtain.

If I knew then what was coming I might have succumbed to the others' insistence to remain in the free world, but I didn't. I believe, however, that our whole life is under God's control. I often wondered what our lives would have been like if we had chosen to stay in Austria, and Vasile told me he thought about that frequently too. When I think of those times I still wonder about the answer. But back then there was no doubt in my mind that we had to go back to our difficult duty. The Lord needed us in that country where the "Beast" was ruling.

When we got back home I hugged Dorinel, I realized he had no idea what we had given up for him.

I was thinking that we had returned for his sake, but it was God's will for us to go back to Romania, and it was His will to grant my husband the grace to suffer for Christ.

Our trip to Vienna remained in my memory like a beautiful dream. But our usual day to day life went on.

An English Family Minibus, Loaded with Bibles

Winter in Bucharest was quite harsh: it was cold, windy and snowy. One year, however, we had a heavy snow that covered everything with such a thick layer that cars could no longer drive on the streets. The ploughs were able to clear only the main avenues. Local authorities had issued a decree forbidding all private cars to drive. Only buses and the cars that took workers to and from work were allowed on the streets.

Children were overjoyed—no school, no homework, only sledding, playing, joy and snowmen everywhere. Mothers could not seem to find their carrots anywhere.

Just then a shipment of Bibles and Christian literature arrived in Bucharest. A couple from England came with a van, along with their baby. They parked on the periphery of the city and then contacted us. I do not know how they managed to reach us under those circumstances. They told us about their van and the large amount of Bibles in it. Vasile didn't know what to do. He could not drive our car because of that decree. Moreover, our car was stuck in deep snow. But he did not have the heart to refuse them. We needed the Bibles, and that family had risked so much bringing them into our country. It was unthinkable to return to England with the Bibles in their van. We had to do something to solve the problem.

Vasile decided to call his brother-in-law, Nelu Man, for help. Nelu was a bus driver and he took the workers from a certain factory to and from work, so he was allowed to circulate. He usually parked the bus in front of his house. This was on Sunday evening.

Vasile and Nelu agreed to meet near where the foreign van was parked. They met in the evening, not too late, because they didn't want to attract attention. Since it was winter it got dark quite early.

The snow made the night glitter like a winter wonderland. The ground was covered in a white carpet and the trees were dressed in white as well. It had stopped snowing and a dreamlike tranquility had settled all around us. The children had gone to bed.

We had to act quickly, so Vasile and I went together. Our foreign brothers had worked all day long to put everything in bags, as Vasile had advised them. When we got there, the bags were ready. Nelu parked his car in front of the van, so the two vehicles were facing each other. They raised the hoods of the cars as if they had some engine problems, then they began to take the bags from the van. They worked on the side of street between the car and the sidewalk. The Englishman brought the bags to the door of his car, Vasile carried them from the van to the bus door, Nelu lifted them inside the bus, and I dragged them into the back of the bus to make room for all the bags.

Everything was going smoothly when suddenly we saw a car coming down the narrow side of the road that was open to traffic. It was a small vehicle, so we realized it could only be the police. We were about to be caught in the act, and if that happened not only us but the missionaries would have been interrogated too.

Vasile and I lay down in the bus. The foreign woman and the child sat on the bags in their van, while her husband and Nelu stood next to the van, looking intently at the engine as if trying to determine what was wrong with the car. The police patrol stopped on the other side of the street. The officer opened the door, put one foot out in the snow, and asked what happened.

"I'm helping him to get his engine started," replied Nelu calmly.

"Then move faster and don't keep the street blocked," said the policeman and he pulled his leg back in the car and drove away.

They had seen a foreign car and had not stopped to search it! That was hard to believe. Meanwhile, on the floor of the bus, Vasile and I had prayed fervently. After the police patrol was gone, we hurried and finished the work. We thanked the foreigners and told them to leave as fast as possible. They had taken a big risk for the Lord and for a foreign nation, while we had risked it for the sake of our own people. We knew, however, that in the Kingdom of God all believers were one. We were all citizens of the same Kingdom.

After the departure of the foreigners, only part of our problem was solved. Now we had to find a storage place for all those Bibles. The bags could not stay in that bus that belonged to the state, because Nelu had to take the workers to the factory by bus the following day. We had to take the bags from the bus that night, and we needed to do it in a central place, where the snow in the streets had been cleared.

Vasile contacted Titus and Minerva, who lived in a downtown apartment and had a cellar for winter supplies. Vasile asked them to allow him to store the bags in their cellar. In order not to be seen by the other residents, we had to wait until they went to bed, but we could not go there too late either, because our activity would have seemed suspicious. There were many heavy bags, and the distance from the street to the basement was pretty far, but we had no choice.

Nelu drove the bus loaded with Bibles right through downtown Bucharest. He could have been pulled over and asked where he was going at that hour. I was afraid, though I tried to be brave. Suddenly the horn of the bus started to honk. After 10 o'clock at night honking was forbidden.

"Nelu, what are you doing? Stop that!"

"I'm not doing anything! I don't know what happened!"

He stopped the bus, got off, disconnected some wires, and the horn was finally silent. The road to our destination seemed so long! Once we arrived at Minerva's place, we waited until the lights in the apartments around us turned off, then we started to work. In the pressure of the moment we could no longer feel the weight of the bags as we carried them to the steps of the cellar, neither did we feel any fatigue. We were glad no one saw us and tried to finish as fast as possible. We were physically and emotionally exhausted, but the joy of doing God's worked surpassed anything.

We were like the children of our congregation who came in small groups to our house every week, in good weather or bad, glad that they could do something for the Lord, no matter how small their contribution was.

We were just as happy, knowing we had been elected to serve this way the believers in the heavenly Kingdom. Where there is love, sacrifice comes easily. Knowing we brought joy to the Lord through our work made us truly happy.

"The Fat Man" and News in the Boots

Several years after we got involved in this underground ministry, Vasile was able to get in touch with a few Christian agencies that were engaged in this work, because missionaries communicated among themselves. We were visited more and more often by foreign ministers.

One spring we were visited by two Americans. One of them was a Mennonite brother named Bontrager, whom we already knew, the leader of a missionary agency from Indiana. His companion was a man we were meeting for the first time. He introduced himself as "The Fat Man", probably his nickname. And indeed we had never seen such a fat man before. He told us with a smile that he was a private investigator and that we could always call him, should we need his services.

On his card were written the following words: *"The Fat Man" – Private Detective*. He was a very nice person. In fact, the two of them told us that they were visiting Romania for a particular reason: "We've learned about the existence of a POW camp that is kept secret in the Soviet Union. Some American prisoners are there, too. We got this information from a Romanian prisoner who managed to escape and return home. We came here to find him but apparently someone made sure the man has simply disappeared in the meantime."

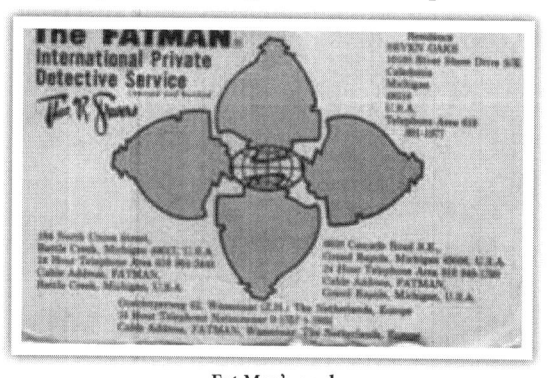

Fat Man's card

We offered the detective some food and tea. When we started drinking the tea, he began pulling from his huge boots a pile of sugar sachets and some small packets of jam. I don't know how he had managed to stuff them all in his boots. He explained that he had taken them from the breakfast meal he had had at the hotel. (Only foreigners could enjoy such goodies; Romanians could get only a certain amount of sugar per month.) After dinner he asked us if we wanted to send something abroad. He assured us that we could count on him; after all, he was not such a good detective for nothing.

Vasile took advantage of that opportunity. We were aware of many difficult situations, persecutions, and fines believers had to pay because they had gathered in houses for prayer. When Vasile heard of such cases, and when he had the chance to communicate the news over the border, they were broadcast by the Free Europe Radio Station and made known to the entire world. Of course the Communists were listening to those programs too, and they had to slow down the persecution, because they wanted to put an end to that negative publicity. Providing the news to that radio station was an effective but risky way of fighting Communist terror. However, if we got caught we would have ended up in jail.

Vasile considered our meeting with "the Fat Man" an excellent opportunity. Who could have been a better emissary than an American detective? Our letters were hidden in his boots. Not long after that we listened with satisfaction to Free Europe Radio Station broadcasting "the news in the boots".

"You must give, if you want to receive"
—John Heasman, the Australian

My husband used to say, "You must give, if you want to receive." We were trying to set some Bible supplies aside for those times when we needed to deliver a larger amount somewhere. We had managed to save a small quantity of Bibles, but we hadn't received more for quite a long time, and that supply was all we had. Vasile remembered his belief, "You must give, if you want to receive." Though I thought it would have been better to keep the scarce supplies we still had, I respected his decision and we gave the books away.

Now we no longer had any Christian materials in Romanian; we had instead a large quantity of Russian Bibles, and some money. After we met Sister Lidia from Chișinău, we made the needs in the Soviet Union known to our foreign contacts. It was much easier for them to bring Bibles into Romania than into the USSR. We hoped to find a way of crossing all that Christian material over the Russian border, and Vasile had a solution in mind. That is how we got all that material.

But as for the Romanian supplies, we didn't have any left. We were used to having lots of Bibles, and we wished we would receive some again. A new shipment arrived soon and the Bible quantity was so large we were amazed that it could get over the border without being tracked.

Some foreign brothers visited Romania with a trailer, like many foreign tourists did. They visited us and Vasile advised them to put all the Bibles in bags, then park their car on a street in our neighborhood, at a certain hour they agreed on. We were going to pass by slowly, in our car, while they were to follow us.

This time, Vasile found a place in a forest close to the city. From the main road to the forest there was a dirt road that we could drive on slowly. As we headed toward the forest, the summer night was already getting dark and the moon was shining brightly. We turned off the lights and drove by moonlight. Once inside the forest we stopped the car in a clearing, turned off the engine and listened in silence to make sure nobody was following us. Then we carried the bags of Bibles from their car to ours. When we were done, we thanked God and our foreign brothers, and then said goodbye. We left the forest separately, for safety reasons.

We were so pleased to get all those Bibles, and even a bit proud thinking of our great deed.

When we reached the road, Vasile turned on the headlights and the tape recorder. We took it with us on all our trips, and most of the songs on it were written by Brother Niculiță Moldoveanu. When we heard the words of one of his songs, inspired from Luke 17:10, they were like a cold shower for us: "And when you've done all you needed to do, you are just an unprofitable servant." We looked at each other and burst out laughing. We had thought we were great. The Spirit of the Lord had to show us the truth: we were not to allow pride to get a hold of us, because it could lead to death.

On another occasion we were visited by an Australian family, John Heasman and his wife, who was pregnant. They came with a van loaded with Christian literature sent by a missionary agency in France. When we downloaded the van we could not believe our eyes. What a large amount of Bibles had been hidden in there!

We could not understand how they had managed to cross the border with all that material, but they told us their car was designed so that they could easily hide lots of things inside. Vasile asked them if they wanted to take the Russian Bibles and money with their van to Chișinău. They agreed.

My husband told them to get a visa for the USSR, but John was sure that they would get it at the border. We had to meet up again, to load the Russian Bibles into their van.

The next day, our Australian friends received the precious cargo and then left. I was a bit nervous for them. That was our first attempt smuggling Russian Bibles over the border. When they returned they told us what had happened:

"We arrived at the Russian border and our van was checked. Everything went well. The customs officers did not find anything. Then they checked our passports and that's when we got in trouble. You were right, Vasile. We needed a visa issued by the Russian Embassy. They told us to apply for one in Bucharest and then they said, 'Nazat'("Go back" in Russian)."

The next day Vasile took them to the Russian Embassy. They filled in the necessary forms and were told to return in 10 days to see if their request was approved or not.

Meanwhile, they went to Bulgaria to solve some other problems. The Bibles were kept in their car, where they were safe. They crossed the Bulgarian border safely and returned later to Bucharest for the visa. Unfortunately, it was denied, and there was nothing they could do about it. So we had to take all those Russian Bibles and money back and say goodbye.

We would have to handle that problem alone and follow a plan Vasile had put together in order to get supplies over the Russian border. We intended to go to Bucovina, a region that bordered Russian Moldova, a Romanian territory occupied by the Russians after WW2.

We wanted to take the Bibles to Grandpa, Vasile's father who lived in Bucovina. Some of the Bibles were in Romanian, and the others in Russian. The latter would be taken by Eusebie to our brothers over the Russian border.

There was a way the Bibles could be smuggled: a believer who worked as a machinist was crossing almost daily from Romania to Russia and back. He used to hide several Bibles wrapped carefully in his tool compartment. A believer on the other side of the border had agreed to pick up the Bibles the Romanian machinist threw out the window in a certain place.

The Bibles could be smuggled over the border quite often, but only several at a time. The accomplices were trustworthy and devout believers.

We decided to carry as many Bibles as possible to Bucovina. Only Vasile and I took that trip, leaving Dorinel with his grandparents.

In Bucovina it had rained a lot and the back roads were very muddy. It was about one kilometer from the road to the house of Vasile's parents. We could not drive all the way up there through the mud, so we took our shoes off, not to lose them in the mud, took the suitcases and started walking. We marched through the deep mud until we reached my in-laws' home.

Grandpa and mother Ghenea were so glad to see us. Even if Vasile was a married man now, to them he was still their beloved baby.

The trip back was a real pleasure. Instead of Bibles, we now carried sweet apples and other goodies from Bucovina, the beautiful garden of Romania.

Cristiana Mihaela

Dorinel used to ask us every year, especially before Christmas, "Please buy me a little brother or sister. That's what I want the most." After six years of waiting his little sister was finally on the way. Dorinel kept on asking when he could play with her. "You need to be patient," we told him. "You can't play with a newborn."

It was not easy to choose a name for the much-anticipated baby sister. No name was good enough for her. We finally picked ten of the names we liked the most, then we drew lots. Even then we were not satisfied, so we settled for Cristiana Mihaela.

I came home from the hospital with a little "doll" wrapped in swaddles and wearing, of course, at least one hat on her head, although it was late August and terribly hot outside. We were afraid she could catch a cold! We put our tiny baby girl in her bed and all of us gathered around her.

She was Dorinel's gift. She had come into the world for his sake—that's what he believed—and for her sake he did everything he could just to make her laugh. He learned to swaddle, to hold her,

Cristiana Mihaela

and to help us bathe her. And as expected, soon her little eyes started watching Dorian everywhere.

Cristiana was a very good baby; she cried neither day nor night. Perhaps the explanation was the fact that the Secret Police had not bothered me while I was pregnant with her, like they had done during my previous pregnancy.

The Lord gave us a peaceful period in our underground ministry of distributing Bibles and other aid. Everything seemed to be going well.

We had no time to waste and we had to organize our schedule wisely, dividing the hours between housework, our jobs, the children's education, our church involvement, prayer meetings in homes, and meetings with foreign missionaries. These were our most important activities, and they all seemed to be well organized. We had begun to feel safe and comfortable. But this was only the calm before the storm.

Dorian was now quite busy with his own responsibilities: school, homework, piano and German lessons, house chores, shopping and walking his baby sister with her stroller.

Cristiana and Dorinel with the stroller   Cristiana

He still had a weakness for Cristiana and when she was one year old, he decided that he would marry her when they grew up. And so he betrayed Aunt Anuța and Brian's daughter, Wendy. Little wonder. With her dark little eyes, her pleated skirt and ruffled top knitted by Sister Leana Ioanid, with her white socks and boots, with her ribbon in her hair, who could have resisted Cristiana? Certainly not Dorinel or her daddy.

They didn't need to be asked twice and were ready to fulfill all her wishes. It was nice to watch them growing together and to see Dorinel holding her small hand, like a protective big brother.

At Solca

We spent our vacations in the mountains or at the seaside. Sometimes we took a trip to Solca in Bucovina. We rented a house there, right next to the park. Sometimes Nelu, Viorica and their five children joined us as well.

That place was a real heaven on earth for the children. There was enough room for them to run and play outside, enjoying the fresh air. They had plenty of good food and fresh fruit. But the number of our days off was limited.

Vasile was working at the Agricultural Academy in Bucharest. Brother Sile Roske was working there too. They were good friends and often had sweet fellowship moments in the Lord.

Brother Sile was the director's right hand, but his true passion was Jesus and His Word. Because he spoke several languages, he had

The Roskes: Sile, Rodica and Ștefănel

opportunities to write and translate many Christian books and articles that were a blessing to many.

Once when Dorinel was sick, Vasile brought me a book about healing written by Oral Roberts and translated by Brother Sile.

While I was sitting next to my sick child who had a fever and was on antibiotics, I read that the Lord could heal when His children prayed with faith. A battle took place in my heart in that moment. I stopped reading and wondered, "Do I have that much faith?" I looked at my son and asked him, "What would you like: to have some shots and get better or to pray with Daddy and Mommy, and be healed?" (What a question!)

"To pray, Mommy."

The three of us got on our knees.

After that prayer Dorian was still feverish. We looked at each other, trying to make a decision. We had to choose between putting the boy (who was about 4 or 5) back to bed, or get him dressed and go out as if he were healthy.

We decided to act according to the confidence in our hearts and we went to visit Aunt Alice because it was her birthday.

Upon returning home the child was perfectly fine. What a blessing was the love of Brother Sile for us and for many, many others. We remained friends with him for life, for better or for worse.

When Cristiana turned three we decided to take her to the kindergarten for the children of the employees of the Agricultural Academy, Vasile's workplace.

We got up every morning and then we split: Dorian went school, I went to work, and Vasile and Cristiana went to the "Academy".

On the way to kindergarten Vasile stopped by to sign the registry book, and then he took Cristiana to the next building.

They left together and returned together. A special bond formed between them. They were spending time together at that sweet age when little girls are so cute and they steal their father's heart forever.

If I ended my story here it would sound like the fairytales in which the prince and the princess lived happily ever after. But if I stopped here how could I explain why we were on that plane, leaving the country with tears of sadness in our eyes?

Beloved Coworkers

My memories kept invading my mind. I remembered some beloved friends who, in their simplicity, were more precious than gold.

One treasured helper was Sister Jeni Bușă. She was as industrious as an ant. We carried lots of heavy bags into her attic on the fifth floor.

Sister Maria Lazăr was a prayer warrior whose inspired words have often guided us.

Tudorel Bratu was a dear brother from the Army of God (a branch of the Orthodox Church).

Brother Tudorel Bratu in Doftea-na, Bacău. His job brought him to Bucharest often. Tudorel was a tall, strong man, with great zeal for his faith. We quickly became friends and whenever he was in Bucharest he spent the night in our apartment. He did not want to go elsewhere, although he could have found other friends to house him. He liked my

Brother Tudorel Bratu and his wife

soup and told me, "Dear sister, I need you to give me a big tablespoon and a jug; the small ones look like toys."

When he came to Bucharest on business he used to leave one day earlier and spend the night with us. The next morning he would go about his business, return in the afternoon, and in the evening he went back home, taking some Bibles with him. Every time he visited us he used to bring different kinds of goodies from the countryside.

Once after he spent the night in our apartment he woke up early in the morning because he had an important meeting with a CEO. He got dressed in the dark, not wanting to wake up our children, and went into the hallway to put his shoes on. He put his shoes on and left. My husband woke up a little later, went into the hallway, and was preparing to leave when I heard him burst into laughter. I went to see what had happened and he told me that Brother Tudorel had accidently taken one of his shoes, though it had a different design and color. I don't know how his day was, but he was very embarrassed when he returned.

We found his misfortune quite amusing. He had entered the director's office, shaken his hand and sat with his legs crossed. When his look fell on his shoes, he froze. He quickly put his feet under the desk in front of him and did not move until he left the office. Only the Lord helped him not to make a fool of himself in front of that director.

We used to spend time together and talk until late at night. Brother Tudorel often asked us lots of questions about our faith. Once he wanted to know, "Why does a person have to be baptized again if he or she was already baptized as an infant?"

We told him the Bible showed clearly that those who believed in Jesus and who were baptized could be saved (Mark 16:16). We explained that babies do not know what's happening to them when they are baptized, and that the godfather could not believe for them. I told him that I had to choose to believe in the Lord Jesus as my personal Savior, not as the Savior of the entire world. After that I asked to be baptized, as a public profession of my faith.

Our words made him think, and we were convinced that once he returned home he would begin searching the Word of God to find out more about baptism. A few years later he asked to be baptized.

One of the guests we were glad to receive in our apartment was Ștefan Viski. He was a student at Bucharest University who stayed in the student dormitory. He spent most of his Saturdays and Sundays with us and often babysat Cristiana so that we could take care of other things.

One day he was accompanied by a young lady who was going to return home to Oradea by train. Ștefan's parents were organizing a youth camp there, and they needed food supplies. We had just received a shipment with lots of food so we decided to send some of it to them by that young lady. Even though she looked like a child, she was a hearty young lady.

Vasile and Ștefan went to the train station early, to carry all the packages to be stored in the hand luggage storage room until the train's departure. Once the luggage was there, they got a receipt. Vasile told Ștefan to keep it, so if he went to the train station earlier, he could take the food parcels and start carrying them to the train.

They separated after that and each one went someplace different. Vasile was the first one to arrive back at the station at the time established for their meeting, before the train's departure. While waiting for Ștefan, Vasile saw the clerk from the luggage department talking to a policeman and gesturing toward him. He realized that the policeman was waiting for him. He was taken to the Police Office and asked to remove everything he had in his pockets. The police officer began to search him. Probably the luggage clerk had reported the case to the authorities, because he had noticed the parcels containing foreign food.

The police officer was looking for the luggage receipt so that he could check the parcels and find out where the food came from. But Ștefan had the receipt. Vasile was upset that he was detained for so long. He was afraid Ștefan would not be able to carry all those parcels to the train. The police officer kept him in his office until the train left. Since he didn't find the receipt he was looking for, he apologized and let my husband go.

Meanwhile Ștefan, who had the receipt, carried the food parcels to the train and everything was fine. Vasile passed by the luggage department just to make sure the food parcels were no longer there. Ștefan had got them all onto the train, and they arrived safely at their destination.

If the police had found that receipt in Vasile's pocket, they would have confiscated the food parcels, because they came from outside the country.

God works in many wonderful ways, but often we do not understand them. Vasile had an understanding with some of his collaborators. They had agreed Vasile would put the Bibles in a parcel and leave that in a storage box at the train station. They used to speak in code about the whole activity.

A brother involved called us saying, "Vasile, I was looking for you last night but I could not find you. I need you to buy me something for my car (he would mention a certain item)."

"I'll try to find it for you. Call me again tomorrow."

"OK. Thank you."

Vasile would get the parcel ready and take it to the luggage storage box from the train station. He would lock the box, using the code they had previously established. He wrote down the number of the box and next day, when his collaborator called again, he asked, "Vasile, did you find what I asked you to?"

"Yes, I did, but I didn't buy it. I didn't know if you were willing to pay so much. It was 127 lei." (127 was the number of the storage box at the train station, where that brother was going to go pick up the Bible parcel.)

"It's good that you didn't buy it. It was too pricey for me, but thank you anyway for the help," said that brother and ended the call.

They had to watch the clock exactly. The parcel could be stored in the box for 24 hours, so it had to be taken before that time was up. Otherwise the box would not open anymore. Then they would have had to go to the clerk of that department, declare the content of the parcel and pay a new fee, and then the clerk would open the box to check it.

Unfortunately they could not declare the content. So they had to be careful not to end up in that situation. Bibles were banned in our country, and if they got caught they could be sentenced to prison.

Liuba's Bravery

Eventually, Vasile had to face such a difficult situation. A brother who came to Bucharest called Vasile speaking the usual code talk. Everything went well up to a certain point, but the man had to stay an extra day in Bucharest. Because he didn't know what to do with the Bibles, he left them in the box until the next day. He probably didn't know about the 24 hours time limit. When he saw he could not open the box he panicked and came to us. Vasile got so upset. He had only two options: abandon the Bible parcels in the box, so no one could find out who put them there, or risk his freedom and declare the contents of the parcels.

Vasile did not want to abandon the Bibles, and the other brother did not want to go to the luggage office and declare the content. Just then Liuba Caravan, Vladimir Caravan's sister, met Basil and learned of the situation. She said she was willing to take the risk because she didn't have a family of her own. Since she insisted she wanted to do it, Vasile decided to go with her to the train station. Once they got there he told Liuba to wait, so he could try to open the box again.

He used the access code and the box opened immediately, but the alarm started sounding too, as if somebody had forced the lock. The police arrived immediately, but he pulled out the heavy bag, put it on his shoulder, and passed right by them without being noticed in the crowd. When he passed by Liuba he whispered to her, "Go right now! Pretend you don't know me!"

He took the bag to our car and drove through some side streets to make sure he was not followed. Only God's angels hid him from the eyes of the police at the train station.

And so, ten years passed like ten days, as the song written by Brother

Niculiță says: "We thought that time was passing, but we were." We thought nothing was going to change as long as our life honored the Lord and He continued to provide His miraculous help.

~ PART EIGHT ~
# Lessons in Faith

The Storm

In the spring of 1975 we received a large shipment of Bibles, New Testaments and Christian literature. One night we carried all those materials to Papa Man. Because of the rain, the entire road was mud. We had agreed to take the books to the end of the paved road, where Papa Man was going to wait for us with his cart. Then we would move the Christian materials onto his cart, and he was going to hide them in his yard.

Meanwhile, we made an inventory of the books we had and a list of the places where we were planning to distribute them. We kept the list in our apartment, as well as one copy of each title. On the last page of the book we had written down the number of copies we had received.

The same week Rodica, the daughter of Brother Fulea from Sibiu, asked us if we could take her home to visit her parents. She was married and lived in Bucharest. We promised we would, and we intended to take some Bibles with us as well. Daniela, the daughter of Brother Niculiță Moldoveanu, was also with us, and she was to go home too. We were to leave on Saturday afternoon.

That Friday evening, we were visited by a brother from outside of Bucharest whom we knew very well, and he asked us to give him some Bibles. Vasile brought them to him and the man left the same night by train. We were glad we didn't have to travel to distribute those Bibles.

Saturday after work we were preparing to leave. Vasile put about one hundred Bibles into the trunk of our car. My mother came to stay with the children so we could go pick up Rodica. We loved going to Sibiu.

The cabbage rolls Sister Lena cooked were memorable, and the songs of Brother Niculiță wonderful. So was our fellowship with Daniela, their daughter.

Right before leaving, the phone rang and Vasile picked up. A "brother" from outside of Bucharest wanted to talk to him.

"Brother Vasile, I'm not from Bucharest and I need to meet you," said that voice.

"I'm sorry, I can't right now, but if you want you can come to us."

"No, brother, I'm not from here and I can't find my way around the city. You come over to me, please. I really have to meet you. I'm near the tower building at Victory Square. I'll hold a newspaper in my hand so that you can recognize me."

Vasile agreed to go, and told me before he left, "Get ready for the trip. I'll just go check and see what this is all about, and I'll be right back." And off he went.

I waited and waited. I did not understand what took him so long. We had such a long trip ahead of us.

After a while I started to worry. He wasn't usually late. One hour passed and he didn't return. After two hours I realized something had happened. If he had been involved in an accident, I would have been contacted by the paramedics. There was only one possibility left, and the thought of it made me shudder. He must have been caught by the Secret Police. And, he had Bibles in the car.

I called Rodica and told her not to come to us after all. I didn't know what to do. I remembered that Eugene, Sister Nina's nephew, had a car and was a member of the Communist Party, so he did not fear the Secret Police as much. I called and asked him to come over.

He arrived right away, and he saw how scared I was. "Let's go to the Secret Police Headquarters to see if your car is parked there. If it is, then you will know for sure where Vasile is."

We drove in his car to the Secret Police Headquarters on Beldiman Street. Our car was parked there. No doubt that Vasile had been caught.

"Oh, Lord, save us for only You can," I whispered.

I knew the Secret Police agents would soon come to search our apartment. We thought that maybe, just maybe, they had not found the Bibles in our trunk. Eugene, an audacious young man, borrowed our car's spare keys, went to the parking lot, got in our car and drove elsewhere. He stopped and checked the trunk; it was empty.

God Sends Brother Gheorghiță

Returning home that evening I tried to control my emotions and thoughts. I sent the kids to my mother. That night, together with Daniela, I started searching all through our apartment, looking for anything that could incriminate us—addresses, letters, Christian literature anything that could prove our relationship with the brethren abroad. God gave me the ability to check everything, so none of that evidence would end up in the hands of the Secret Police.

We had one copy of every Christian book we had received and a list with the names of all those who were to receive the materials. But the list was missing; Vasile had it with him. That meant the Secret Police had it now. This realization was another severe blow for me.

Once I finished gathering all the compromising evidence in our apartment, I had two bags full of papers. It was early in the morning. I put the bags by the door, not knowing what to do with them. I could not hide them at my parents' or neighbors' place.

Brother Gheorghiță Boeru

"God, where should I go?" I asked the Lord. Suddenly the doorbell rang. The Secret Police agents would not have used the doorbell. I went to the door to see who it was, and to warn them to leave immediately to avoid suspicion. I opened the door and saw Brother Gheorghiță Boeru.

Standing in the doorway, he asked, "Pușa, what can I do for you?"

How did he know I needed help? Who had sent him? I didn't have time to explain what had happened so I just told him, "Please, take these bags and hide them somewhere."

Brother Gheorghiță took the bags and left right away. He did not even enter our apartment.

Only a few minutes later Vasile and the Secret Police were at the door. Three or four men rudely burst into our apartment and began rummaging through all our stuff. But the apartment had already been "turned upside down" by me. However, they found and seized several items, such as Vasile's razor, a tape recorder, the New Testament I kept in my bag, etc.

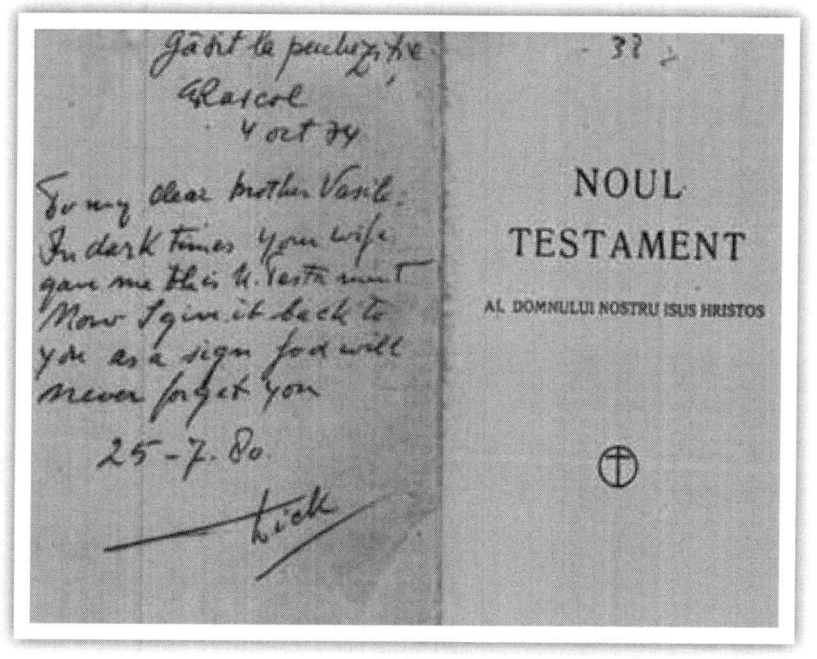

A New Testament

After several hours of searching, the Secret Police agents left, telling Vasile he was scheduled for a new interrogation the following day.

Meanwhile we received word from the brother to whom we had given some Bibles the previous day, and we understood what had happened.

The Secret Police had searched all the luggage in the night train he was in (at that time some anticommunist leaflets and pamphlets had been found in trains and other places). During that raid the police officers found the Bibles in his suitcase and took him to their headquarters. They asked him where he had got the books from. After they threatened him, he told them Vasile's name. That was when the Secret Police went into action. One of their officers pretended to be the believer who called Vasile, asking to talk to him face to face. The plan was to make him leave our apartment, seize him and take him to their headquarters, and interrogate him to find out where he got the Bibles.

In Victoria Square, when Vasile was supposed to meet the "brother" he spoke with on the phone, he was met by two Secret Police agents, Stănescu and Iagăr. They escorted him to their headquarters. There they searched our car and found some Christian literature and about one hundred Bibles that were intended to be distributed in Sibiu. Everything matched the information received from the brother they had caught on the train.

Vasile told me, "I've been questioned all night long by three groups of officers. They wanted to know where I got the Bibles from and the names of the people involved in our network.

I prayed all the time, not knowing how to answer without getting anyone else into trouble. I prayed, "Lord, You promised in Your Word that You would teach us what to answer when we are questioned by the authorities. Lord, teach me too."

Because he didn't receive a word from the Lord, he kept silent. The officers yelled at him angrily, but they could not get anything out of him. They even quoted passages from the Bible suggesting that he should be subject to the state's authorities, and they hit him in the head with a Bible.

He was silent the whole time, and silence was the best answer. He kept on thinking of the copies we had at home and the numbers written on each of them. If they found that evidence they would have eventually discovered the main storage place where we kept lots of materials. He didn't know what had happened at home.

After the all night interrogation, three Secret Police agents escorted him to our apartment intending to search it. When their car reached our street, Vasile saw Brother Boeru coming from the direction of our apartment. He was afraid, and turned his eyes elsewhere so that the Secret Police agents would not realize he knew Brother Boeru.

I asked Brother Gheorghiță later, "What made you come to me right then? Just a few moments after you took those bags the Secret Police came to search our apartment. They would have got all the evidence in those bags if you had arrived only a few minutes later."

"I was praying," he replied, "and suddenly felt a strong urge in my heart, saying to me: *Go to Pușa right now. She needs you. She needs help.* So I left immediately. I didn't know what that was all about, so that's why I asked what I could do for you."

Difficult days followed for our family, and our life has never been the same. The Secret Police were in front of our apartment day and night. (What a miserable job—staying on the street and watching every move people make.) We were followed everywhere. No one could visit us without becoming a suspect too, and nobody wanted to be questioned by the Secret Police.

We had to inform the foreign ministries we were working with not to send anyone or anything to us. Everyone must now avoid us.

Meanwhile the underground work had to continue, but we needed to find another way of doing it. Trying to keep a low profile, we continued our "normal" daily routine. We went to work, came back home, took the kids for walks in the park or to visit my parents or a few other friends who were not at all involved in our ministry. And of course we were summoned to and interrogated by the Secret Police agents on a daily basis. They kept on threatening us that we would be sentenced to prison.

I prayed that the Lord would deliver us. I loved to read the Bible story of the angel that delivered Peter from prison. However, when I read the Scripture looking for comfort, most of the time I came to passages about Joseph who was sold by his brothers and then ended up in an Egyptian prison. I tried to read something else, not wanting to think of prison, but the thought kept haunting me. Then I told myself: "No, God will not allow that! We served the Lord with a pure heart. He will step in and save my husband!"

And yet the image of Joseph, who was thrown into prison even though his heart was pure, persisted in my mind. The Lord was trying to prepare me for something, but I refused to understand. I wanted my will to be God's will too, and I fought with all my power for that. Therefore I could not receive any comfort or advice from anyone. I kept on thinking that my will was the display of my faith.

Dorinel was a big boy now and he understood the situation. He had figured out the places the Secret Police used for watching us, and he recognized their cars. When he rode his bike in the street he noticed their presence.

We needed to send word to our foreign network about our situation, yet we didn't know how to do it because the Secret Police were watching us day and night.

One day we found out that a missionary family was ready to carry our informative letter. They told us that they would be close to our apartment in a certain place, at a certain time. We had to get there without being followed, but that seemed impossible. The Secret Police agents were at the gate. Daniela, the daughter of Brother Niculiță Moldoveanu, had come to us the very same day. She had come to Bucharest for some exams.

Her family had been through similar circumstances, and her dad had spent many years in prison. She had come to encourage and to

With Daniela Moldoveanu in Herăstrău Park

assure us that they were by our side.

When most people avoided us, fearing for their own safety, such a kind display of friendship was most valuable.

Daniela resembled me closely, and she was about the same height, so we had an idea. When it got dark outside, she put on some of my clothes and arm in arm with Vasile she got in our car and they left together. We were hoping to convince the Secret Police agents that Vasile and I had gone somewhere.

Dorinel was hiding in the street to see what happened. The Secret Police car immediately followed ours. Then Dorinel came and told me that no one was watching our apartment anymore and the street was clear. I went downstairs with the letter, took it to the missionary family that was waiting for me, and returned home as quickly as I could. After a while Vasile returned as well. It had worked.

Our news reached its destination. Through this the believers in the free world learned what "religious freedom" in Communist countries was really like. They were also warned not to bring any food aid or Christian materials to us, because the Secret Police would have caught them immediately.

Most of our friends found out about the surveillance we were under, but there was one isolated case when a brother from Israel, Izi Bal, a friend of Sister Anuța, came to us with some humanitarian aid. He parked his car not far from our apartment, got out and walked along the street, trying to find our address. He was on our street and looking at the house numbers. I was outside with the children and Vasile was returning from the Secret Police Headquarters, accompanied by an agent.

We were all on the sidewalk when we saw that brother looking at our building's number. The agent asked him immediately, "What number are you looking for?"

"Number 12."

"This is the number 12, he said. Who are looking for?"

"Vasile Răscol," he answered.

"I am Vasile," said the agent.

We looked at him, astonished by his insolence. Vasile stepped in right away and cleared things up. "He is Iagăr, a Secret Police agent, not Vasile Rășcol. I am Vasile and I'm being interrogated by this agent."

Our poor guest was very scared, but it was too late. The agent took him to our apartment and searched him. He wanted to know why he had come to us. Although he was scared, he made the agent understand that he had only brought us greetings from some friends in Israel who had left Romania a few years ago. To our relief, he was finally allowed to leave.

Exasperated that they could not get any information from Vasile after several weeks of intense interrogation, the Secret Police agents threatened him that he would be sentenced to prison, where they had their means of making him talk and telling them everything they wanted to know.

Vasile's court date was finally settled. The news spread like wildfire among Romanian and foreign believers. It was the first time a Romanian was to be judged for possessing Bibles, and the first official trial for that charge. At the beginning of the Communist era, people were thrown into prison by the thousands. Many political prisoners were killed. The rich were sent to labor camps, and the faithful spent many years in prison, and all without any explanation.

Now, in our time, the government wanted to prove that Romania respected the rights of its citizens in order to gain political, economic and international recognition. Thus the authorities had to take into consideration the public opinion of the international community.

The news of the persecution that had been spread abroad and also had been broadcast by the Free Europe Radio Station enraged the Romanian rulers. It limited their ability to persecute the Church. They did not care if their own people lived in terror. They only cared that their image was tarnished.

For our people it was hard to bear the difficult situation in our country, but the most difficult of all was the fact that we had to sing songs of praise to our oppressors. Although we were theoretically free, we lived as if imprisoned. The whole country was a prison.

The authorities could have arrested Vasile and simply made him disappear, but they wanted to teach others a lesson, and prove at the same time that Romania had the legal structure of a civilized country.

Communist Justice

The day of the trial arrived and I was convinced that the Lord was going to miraculously deliver Vasile. However, deep in my heart, the Spirit of the Lord was telling me that Vasile was going to have the same fate as Joseph, who was sold by his brothers and ended up in prison. I tried to dismiss that feeling and didn't tell anyone about it. I thought it was just a personal fear.

Brother Niculiță Moldoveanu and his family, Sister Lena and their daughter Danicla, came to be with us. They understood our situation better than others, because they had gone through it as well.

On the morning of the trial, before going to the court, Sister Lena said, "Pușa, it would be good to get a suitcase ready for Vasile, with some clothes and food in it, and take it with you."

I got upset and rebuked the others for their lack of faith. My confidence made me deaf to the advice of others. Vasile, on the other hand, was surrounded by different opinions of different people. Only he could hear the voice of his own heart. Many believers were praying for him day and night.

During his interrogation he had been strong and wise. None of those he worked with was investigated or arrested. The Secret Police had not found out anything else, or discovered any other Bibles, except for the ones in the train and in our car. They were angry and kept on threatening him.

I was praying that "my will" be done. But the Lord was silent. My prayers ascended only up to the ceiling of our apartment, and that feeling made me so sad.

Hundreds of believers from all denominations came to the trial. They all stood outside, waiting for the doors to open. When they did, there was not enough room inside for all of them. Those who could not enter waited outside.

We had hired two lawyers. One of them had some knowledge about Christians and their faith, while the other was well known. (How could I imagine they would be able to change anything?)

The trial ended quickly, and it didn't seem to make any sense. Each of the parties involved said something. The "Christian" lawyer asked for mercy. The famous lawyer mentioned there was no law that prohibited the possession of Bibles. However, the prosecutor insisted that Vasile was definitely guilty.

Finally, the judge pronounced the sentence: two years in prison for distributing Bibles without a legal permit. We could read on the judge's face the contempt for his own job. He did not have a choice about the sentence. He had not even read the documents in Vasile's file.

Uproar filled the courtroom. People began to protest. My father tried to get Vasile out of their hands. I was standing by him as if hit by lightning. To avoid the crowd, the guards grabbed Vasile and pushed him toward the back door. Without my knowledge, Daniela had packed some clothes for Vasile and managed to hand him the suitcase.

I was petrified. The pain in my heart became unbearable. In spite of feeling broken, I became like a lioness. They had taken my husband! No, I will not let them! I will fight for him as long I have life in me! Lord, why did You allow this? Haven't I been through this agony with my dad? Now it's about my husband and the father of my children!

I had totally forgotten about Joseph and his trials. I learned that Vasile was to be taken to the police office in our district until his documents were filled in, and after that he was going to prison. I hurriedly bought some food and took it to him. There I saw Vasile chained next to another inmate. My heart was torn to shreds.

I had to tell something to our children, who had been staying with my mother. Dorinel was old enough to hear the truth. Cristiana was too young to understand why her beloved daddy was no longer home. I told her only, "Daddy is gone on a business trip." She knew that her dad was going quite often on business trips, and he always brought her a toy when he returned.

It was as if the life was draining out of me. A great sadness rolled over me and I forgot that we were given grace to suffer for Christ. I had thought only about us, saying, "God, we've served You with a pure heart. Why did You allow this?"

Afterward I requested an audience with the judge. Incredibly, he received me. I didn't care what happened to me, and said fearlessly, "How could you condemn an innocent man to prison? You have not even opened his file. You don't even know why you declared him guilty. Since when is the Bible a dangerous book, when all human civilization is based on it? Look, I have brought you a Bible to read it so that you can understand what it is about."

The judge looked at me with pity in his eyes and said, "You're right, but there's nothing I can do. The decision was made at a higher level. Don't try to change it—it's impossible. No one can do anything about it."

He accepted the Bible, the very same book that had made him utter the sentence that took my husband to prison.

Hearing the word "impossible", hope lit up in my heart again. I took courage. "Impossible ... the decision was taken at a higher level ... " How high could that level be? Was there anything impossible with the Lord? Was anyone higher? Then I knew in my heart that God would manifest His power for His glory, and stopped thinking about my will or desire. I was jealous for the glory of God. I knew that the Lord would not allow the pride and arrogance of men to rule, no matter how "high" they thought they were. If the judge had not used the word "impossible" maybe the situation wouldn't have been so, but when he said a definite "impossible" he opened the door for God's miraculous intervention. I felt it in my heart in spite of the hostile circumstances we were in.

But the painful, heartbreaking reality was still present. The only prayer I said day and night was, "Lord, do a miracle and bring Vasile home for our sake."

And nothing happened. A deep sadness filled my heart. I became indifferent to everything else. I fulfilled all my obligations mechanically. Whether I was at work or at home, I was thinking all the time about how to help Vasile.

Neculai, my husband's younger brother, was a great support for me during those days.

He was even more outraged than I was and always ready to do something. There must have been a reason for the meaning of our last name. In Romanian, Răscol means "uprising".

Neculai

Lots of petitions, protests, hearings and visits followed, as well as lots of money given to different people, hoping that would help.

Brothers of faith from other Christian denominations signed a petition requesting Vasile's release or their arrest, because they were guilty of the same crime of having received Bibles. Brotherly unity was unprecedented.

The official reason for Vasile's conviction was the receiving and distribution of Bibles and religious literature. By sending him to prison the authorities wanted to teach all other Christians a lesson, and also to force Vasile to identify all the other members of his network. However, the country's Constitution did not incriminate such an act. The Constitution declared freedom of religion, and the authorities did not anticipate the huge reaction that followed. They had made a mistake by mentioning the true reason for sending Vasile to prison, and they never repeated it again. Other Christians who were imprisoned afterwards were sentenced for fictitious reasons.

The protests that took place abroad were intense, but we only found out about them and their effects later.

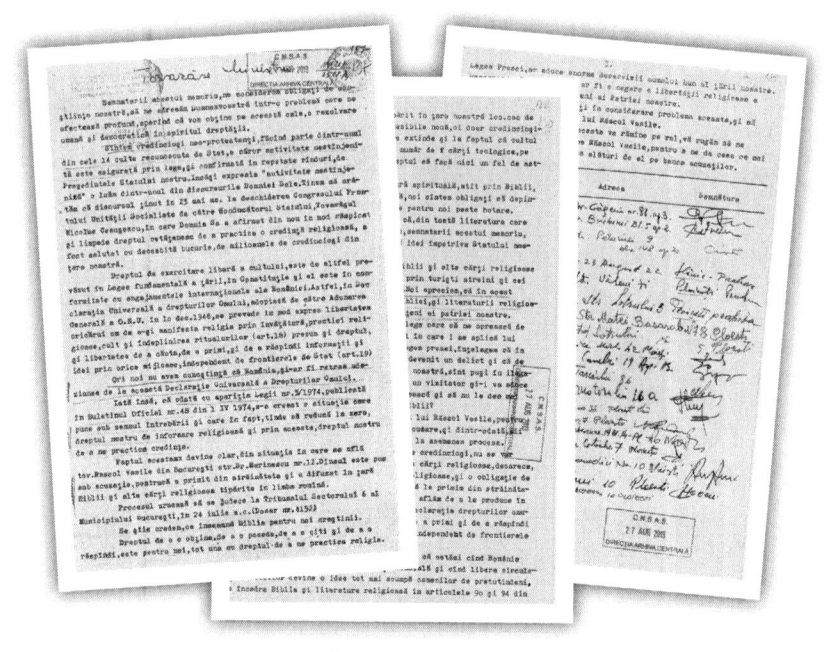

Petition with signatures (see Appendix 1)

Just as the Secret Police agents had threatened, they kept Vasile in their prison after his arrest for intense interrogation.

Since the Bibles they had found were not printed in Romania, it meant they must have come from abroad, having been smuggled by someone with the help of a whole network of people. They wanted to identify everyone involved in the process.

Vasile was held there for six months without being allowed to contact anyone. He could not be visited, send or receive any letters, or get any news from outside. I tried to get to him, but was not allowed.

For six months I had no news about him. Besides, the continual harassment I was subject to was meant to make me give in. I was often interrogated as well and the Secret Police agents would say to me, "Vasile has already told us everything. Here are his statements. We know it all. Do not try to hide anything. Confess now!'

"If you know everything, why do you keep on asking me about it? I do not know anything."

The pressure and the nightmare one goes through under interrogation by such people are hard to express. The very words "interrogation at the Secret Police office" were synonymous with "terror". I never knew if I would be allowed to return home to my children.

One morning, the children and I were awakened around five by a loud thump on the door, as if someone had kicked it with their foot. I jumped out of bed and went to see who it was. When I opened the door, four Secret Police agents rushed inside. Scared, the children had got out of bed too. I ran to them to calm them down, though I was just as scared.

The agents had come to search our apartment. I already knew what that meant. The thump on our door had woken up our neighbors, too. Because the agents needed some witnesses, they brought in Mr. and Mrs. Andreescu, our next door neighbors.

They did not even allow me to get dressed. I barely managed to put on a dressing gown. Mrs. Andreescu asked their permission to return to her apartment because she was ill. I finally convinced them to allow Cristiana, who was only four, to go with her. So only Dorinel and I were left there. My son proved to be very brave, and at the same time an important support and help for me.

The agents kept searching all over the place and whenever they found something they thought might be of interest they placed it on the table. I had a notebook with addresses and phone numbers I did not want to get into their hands. It would have caused more interrogations. I exchanged a look with my son and he understood he should try to take it to Mrs. Andreescu. And so he did.

The agents turned our entire apartment upside down. They rolled up the rug, took the paintings off the walls, moved our beds and turned our mattresses. They checked everything—the stove, the toilet, the kitchen. Nothing escaped their searching eyes. I had a small New Testament and a hymn book they took that day. I had to write on them "found during the search."

They had probably become desperate in their failed attempts to discover some kind of conspiracy against the socialist order.

After three or four hours they were almost done and ready to write their report, when Brother Sile Roske appeared in the doorway. I had totally forgotten it was the day when he came to tutor Dorian in German.

I prayed silently, "Oh, Lord, don't allow him to get into their hands!"

The Secret Police agents wanted to know who he was and why he had come, but for reasons that remained unknown to me they left in a hurry. They did not insist on finding out anything from Brother Sile, and off they went.

I was left there alone, humiliated and sad, thinking of Vasile. I wondered how he was doing. At least I was home and "free" to stay with my children.

From that day on Dorian did not want to sleep alone in his room anymore. I took him into my room and the three of us started sharing it together.

Cristiana kept on asking me, "Mother, when is Daddy coming back from the business trip?" And I tried to reassure her that he would come soon.

One day, when Nelu my brother-in-law came over, Cristiana asked, "Uncle Nelu, would you like to be my daddy? I see my daddy is not coming home from the business trip anymore."

The words of my four-year-old daughter broke my heart. How could she possibly understand what was really going on?

What a wonderful thing it is to have a daddy around. I cannot understand how so many families split up, not even considering all the suffering the children left behind go through.

One night, after Cristiana fell asleep, Dorian asked me, "Mama, Daddy is watched by guards there, isn't he?"

"Yes, he is," I said.

"Mom, let's not eat for one month, so we can save all that money and go pay the guards to let Daddy come home!"

Oh, the innocence of a child's heart. How could I hold back my tears after hearing such words?

A few months had passed since Vasile had been taken away, and we still did not know anything about each other.

A New Oath

One day at work I was told about a new decree demanding all employees with a university degree to sign a declaration that they would follow all the decisions of the Communist Party, whether they were party members or not. That statement was required in order to keep one's job. So if I didn't want to lose mine, I had to sign that statement.

I had to deal with a new challenge now. Signing that statement would mean that I agreed with the Communist principles, and one of them stated there was no God.

How could I possibly sign such a paper? I believed not only in God, but also in Jesus my Savior, whom I loved wholeheartedly. How could I agree to fight for the fulfillment of the Communist doctrine? It would have been as if I was denying my faith.

Anxiety filled my heart. Vasile was in prison and I had to support the children on my own. If I did not sign that paper I would lose my job and all the means of providing for my family. If I did sign it in order to keep my job, I would have made a compromise. These thoughts were a constant dilemma for me.

The day when all the employees had to sign the statement was approaching, and I still did not know what to do. I was praying to the Lord, "God, You know I'm your child and I love You. If I sign that paper it doesn't mean I support what it says. I would do it just to keep my job and provide for my children." But somewhere deep down the Spirit of the Lord was telling me: "You have to choose now between Me and your job."

"But Lord, I have no choice. You can surely understand that, while they can't," I argued.

Still, the Lord's answer was the same: "You have to choose between

Me and your job."

I had no peace in my heart. This was my own trial and I had to face it alone. Nobody could help me or give me any advice.

I remember clearly what happened next. My workmates and I left the lab and headed for the principal's office in the building next door. All the leaders of the Geological Institute were there, as well as the party secretary. We were supposed to go in one by one and sign the statement. It was a formality. My turn was coming and I still did not know what to do.

All of a sudden I had a saving idea. I decided to sign the paper after I added a paragraph to it, stating I would not do anything against my religious beliefs.

As I entered the office, the paper was put in front of me and I was asked to sign it. To everybody's surprise, I opened my mouth and said, "Comrade director, I want to sign the statement and I agree with everything it says except for one little mention—I will never do anything that is against my faith. I am a Christian. So please allow me to add one paragraph about this on my statement and then I will sign it."

After a moment of silence that seemed an eternity, the director shouted outraged, "Comrade, you must sign the statement just the way it is. You cannot add anything to it."

"Then I can't sign it." These words came out of my mouth without even thinking, as if someone else was talking for me. That moment something extraordinary happened. My whole being was flooded with a joy I had never felt before.

I left the "comrades" right there and left the room with a song of praise in my heart; I returned to the lab almost jumping with joy like a child. I was so happy, even though I knew exactly what was going to happen to me. It was as if I had lost my mind.

When my colleagues heard what happened they tried to help me by talking to our superiors to allow me to keep my job. Their friendship and love touched me. They knew I had to provide for my children all alone. My peace and joy were a complete surprise for them. In fact, I was just as amazed.

But after a while that state of wonder and happiness passed, and I had to face the harsh reality. As expected, I was fired. With polite apologies my bosses told me that they had to respect the law. Otherwise their own jobs would have been in danger, and I knew they were right.

So I stayed at home with no job, no husband and no hope of earning any money. But now I had more time. I had time to ponder my circumstances, including all the troubles that worried me and brought despair to my heart.

Mysterious Messengers

I tried to stay by myself for as long as I could, not wanting others to see the despair and sadness mirrored on my face. One evening, when the children were with my parents and I was home alone, through constant tears I prayed, "Lord, how am I going to survive from now on with no income? I'm no good anymore. I can't provide for my children, I have no job, I can't help Vasile, and I can't get involved in the ministry either. Why should I keep on living? Lord, take my life too!" (How easily I succumbed to the hardships.)

I don't know when I fell asleep crying. Later, I was awakened by a knock on the door. It was not the noisy way the Secret Police agents announced their presence, but a soft knock. Who could it be at this late hour, I wondered. I didn't know exactly what time it was and I didn't even care. I was too heartbroken.

At the door were two young women smiling at me. I invited them into the small hallway. They came in and asked me in English, "Mrs. Răscol?"

I said yes. They handed me an envelope, said goodbye, smiled at me, and left.

It all happened in only a few moments. I didn't have time to say anything, or invite them in, or ask them who they were and why they had come. They were gone as unexpectedly as they had arrived.

I returned to my bedroom and opened the envelope. There was some money inside. I counted the bills and began to cry. The amount was the equivalent of two months' pay. Weeping and ashamed, I thought, "How could I doubt the Lord's provision? God, please forgive me!" Then I told myself, "Though I was in the hands of men, the Lord came to my rescue. But what would have happened if I had been afraid of people and signed that statement rejecting God? Who could have saved and cared for me?"

I gave glory to Him for His great goodness, because He did not abandon me in my weakness.

The Lord asks us just to have faith, trust and patience. This is how His saints are tested. They have to prove patience in times of trial, and patience was a virtue I was missing.

You might think the equivalent of two months' pay is easily spent when one has to pay the rent, other bills, buy food, and cover all the other necessities. But the miracle was that the Lord took care of us in the most unexpected ways. Even the neediest believers stopped by to say a word of encouragement and to leave a bag full of goodies, for which they had spent the little money they had, and had stood in line for hours to buy. If I tried to protest they would say, "Just think that this comes from the Lord."

Vasile's older brother Ionel would often bring us food supplies, even sometimes from expensive restaurants. Neculai, my youngest brother-in-law, was more than a brother to me. He brought us food from Bucovina and accompanied me wherever I went in my attempts to help Vasile. He even risked his own freedom by getting past the president's guards and trying to hand a petition to Ceaușescu! I was not alone, and this made my burden seem easier.

Letters of encouragement (see Appendix 2)

Vasile's situation became well known outside Romania, as I began to understand when I started receiving encouraging letters from abroad. It became evident that many people were praying for us and organizing protest rallies in front of Romanian embassies in free countries.

I was receiving letters from England, Switzerland, Holland, Germany, Norway, America, Japan, Argentina and other places.

It was a real miracle. How were those letters allowed to reach me? Censorship was very strict. The letters had been checked, since some of them were opened when they arrived. It was great to know that I was not alone, forgotten and abandoned. At the same time the Free Europe Radio Station broadcast news and messages about my husband's arrest. The comfort and courage I received gave me strength to go on, and I kept on sending petitions to the authorities.

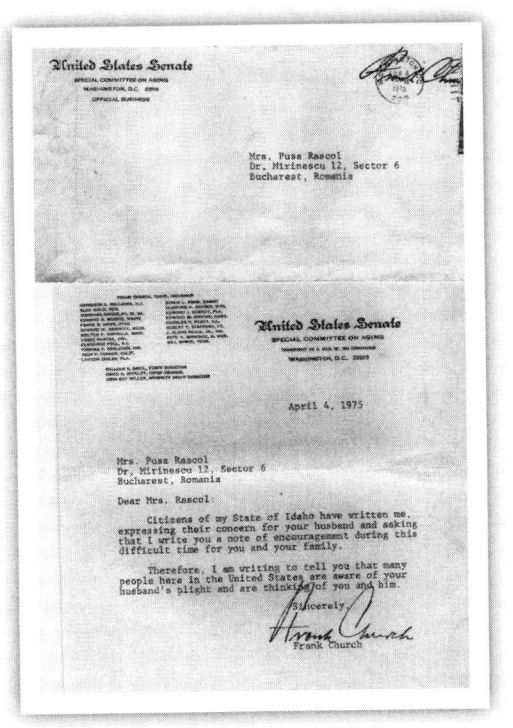

see Appendix 2

Six months had passed since Vasile's arrest and I still didn't know anything about him.

~ PART NINE ~
Freedom's Promise

The Appointment

Finally, after six months, I was told that Vasile had been transferred from the Secret Police prison to the prison of Rahova, where I was allowed to visit him.

I was very excited. After half a year I was going to finally meet my husband, but I could not bring him any hope. How was I going to tell him that I had not been able to help him in any way? It wouldn't do him any good to hear about all the petitions and interventions, about the money given to the lawyer, about the visits to the residence of the president, or about Neculai's attempting to personally hand a petition to Ceaușescu himself. The letters about his situation that had been sent abroad and the news broadcasted by the Free Europe Radio Station that urged the audience to send letters of protest to the Romanian government did not help him either. He was still in prison, while I had not solved anything and I could not see the light at the end of the tunnel.

I did not know what else I could do, and everything I had already tried was of no avail.

I wondered how my husband was. What had the system turned him into? How was it going to be when we would face each other through the bars? I had already had a similar experience with my father for six years.

And yet, I had to be strong. I had to go and encourage him just as I had been encouraged. I had to give him hope. "Oh Lord, have mercy on both of us," I prayed.

Words are often useless. Just being in the presence of your loved one, looking in his eyes, understanding that you are loved regardless of the circumstances is better than words. This is what I could do for Vasile, and what I needed to get from him as well.

The meeting was going to last only for a few minutes, and of course we were listened to and watched all along. Under those circumstances we could not say much—just a few short, to the point questions.

"I'm glad to see you. How are you?"

"OK. How are you?"

"OK." (I didn't say anything about losing my job, because I didn't want him to worry.)

"How are the kids?"

"They miss you, and they want to see you."

"Don't bring them here. I don't want them to see their father behind bars. How are the brothers doing?" (He wanted to know if other believers had been arrested too.)

"They are all OK. They are praying for your situation."

Now it was my turn to ask, "How are you doing here?"

"They put me in a cell with the most dangerous people, he replied sadly. No guard dares to enter there alone; they come only in groups with rifles in their hands, ready to shoot. You never know if you are going to survive or be mutilated by the cellmates. They fear no one. It's awful to be with them in the same cell day and night."

His words broke my heart. I left the prison with a huge weight on my chest. I decided to request an appointment with the warden of the prison and ask him to move my husband from that cell.

I requested an appointment, and I waited. All my previous requests had been denied so far. The petitions were the only instrument I could use. To my surprise and joy, I received permission to meet the warden.

That day, I went to his office long before the scheduled time. I sat there, nervously thinking what to tell him. He must have been a tough man to be able to handle such a job. He was dealing with criminals of all kinds, and of course most of them claimed to be innocent. What could

I tell him to earn his favor?

While waiting in the lobby to be invited in, I was troubled by all these concerns. Then suddenly a thought came to my mind: "We are in the hands of our Lord, not in the hands of men. I must tell Him all about it." That moment I felt that Jesus was right there with me at the door. My eyes filled with tears and I began to praise the Lord while an unusual peace came over me.

I heard somebody calling my name and I entered. Quietly but with no fear in my heart, I sat on the chair the warden pointed me to, near the door. I looked at the man behind the desk, across the room, waiting for him to lift his eyes and look at me.

"What do you want? Why did you request an audience?" he asked me after a while.

"Sir, I certainly cannot say anything different than all those others who request an appointment. And perhaps I was naïve to hope that you will take heed of my words. However, since I'm here, I would ask you to do me favor, to check the record of my husband and look at his picture that must be inside. Just look at his eyes. You are an experienced man. Are those the eyes of a criminal or of an evil and dangerous man? You are not responsible for his sentence; you were not the one who convicted him. He was found guilty for distributing Bibles to Christians. So he ended up in this prison that you manage, and I'm asking you: Why is he locked in a cell with the most dangerous men? Why can't he serve his time like any other inmate? He has not seen his family, or even the sunlight, for six months while he was in the custody of the Secret Police, and now he is here under these terrible circumstances."

After some silence, he raised his eyes from my husband's record, took a look at me and said with a gentle voice, "What do you want me to do for him? Ask me anything that is in my power and it will be done."

I heard my own words like in a dream. "Please move him to a more humane environment. I'd like him to be able to go out and get some fresh air, to see his children—not behind bars, but in a different room where he can embrace them. And I don't want him to appear in front of them dressed in the prison uniform. I'd like to buy a toy for our little girl and hand it to him, so that he can give it to her as a gift. The children know that he is gone on a business trip."

The warden looked at me smiling and he said, "Very well, so be it. Bring some food, too."

In my purse was a New Testament I'd brought for him. I got up, drew near his desk and placed the New Testament in front of him. I reached my hand out to him and gave him a thankful look. I was not able to speak. Tears of gratitude filled my eyes, because the Lord had allowed me to find such favor in the eyes of that man.

When I got back home I told the children, "We're going to see Daddy."

"Shall we bring him home?" Dorinel asked me.

"No, we'll just go see him."

I saw joy mixed with sadness in his eyes. Cristiana wanted us to go right away. I had to calm her down. "Just wait a little longer and then we'll go."

As I had requested of the warden, I bought a beautiful doll and some other toys, and on the scheduled day we went to meet Vasile. We were all excited. I was wondering if indeed the warden would keep his promise. I had decided not to take the kids with me to Vasile behind the bars, in case the warden did not keep his word. I did not want to humiliate my husband. All these thoughts passed through my mind on the way to jail.

It was a beautiful summer day, like the ones we used to spend with our children playing in the mountain groves, or taking hikes, looking for fragrant wild strawberries during summer vacations. Our children, especially Cristiana, seemed like little bear cubs looking for honey.

The great event of this summer trip was the blessing of seeing Daddy and enjoying those moments together, for only God knew when his "business trip" was going to end.

Once we arrived at the prison I handed the toys to a guard. They had found out about our arrangement and realized they had to treat Vasile nicely, as if he wasn't an inmate. I noticed the surprise on their faces, but also their pleasure in displaying some goodness. Perhaps some of them had children at home as well. I thought maybe the warden was secretly watching our little setup for our family reunion.

We were taken to an office where we sat in a corner and waited. After a long time I saw Vasile coming. He was skinny and pale, and his red eyes showed he had been crying. He was still fighting back tears.

As he entered, with his shirt on, not the prison uniform, he stopped at the other end of the room with the bag of toys in his hand, without taking any step, as if petrified.

We were looking at each other across the room. For a few moments, the children wondered who that stranger was. Finally, I was able to tell the kids, "Go to Daddy!"

Dorian decided to be brave and stepped forward. Cristiana was scared; she did not recognize her daddy and held on tightly to me.

"It's all right," I said to her, and I ran to give Vasile a hug. Soon the kids relaxed and finally climbed up in his arms. The ice had been broken. Vasile collected himself too and was able to enjoy our moments together.

(Some time later I found out why we'd had to wait so long. When Vasile was told about our visit, just minutes before we got there, he started crying so hard that he could not control his emotions. The guard told him to calm down and explained what the visit was about. Vasile went to the bathroom to wash his face and then he came to meet us.)

Visiting time was running out and I did not want us to push it. We told each other we would meet again soon and said goodbye. None of us knew how long that was going to be. But at least I knew where Vasile was, and I could go visit him from time to time, though not under the same special circumstances.

Next day, Cristiana spoke only about her daddy, about his business trip, and of course about the doll she had received from him.

A few days later, Viorica, Vasile's sister and her children came to see us. Liliana, her little girl who was about the same age as Cristiana, could not take her eyes off the doll.

"Cristiana, do you think you can let me play with your doll too?" she asked.

"Liliana, I can give her to you for just a little while. Daddy gave her to me. But you can ask your daddy to go on a business trip and buy you one."

We all laughed because nobody wanted Nelu to leave on such a "business trip".

Encouraging Letters and Prayers

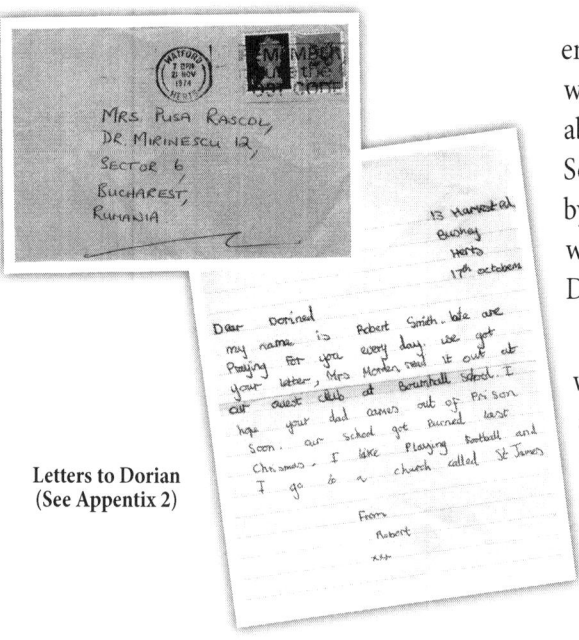

The number of encouraging letters we received from abroad increased. Some were written by children who were close to Dorian's age.

I read the letters with my children and we prayed for those who had written them. We were grateful for all those children in the free world who took the time to think of and write to people who were less fortunate, and to comfort those in need. I wanted my children to grow up in the same spirit.

Letters to Dorian (See Appentix 2)

We were in the prayers of many, and the solidarity chain spread like wildfire in dry stubble.

the Bunica family

One day we were visited by the Bunica family from Brașov. A beautiful friendship with lots of precious memories connected us.

The city of Brașov is situated in the center of the country, and on our frequent trips around Romania distributing Bibles, we sometimes spent the night in their home. Every time our stopovers turned into a delicious meal, and we often got food supplies for the rest of our trip. We felt at home under their roof. Once we were driving to Sibiu, and the Popescus were with us when we stopped by our friends in Brașov. This time no one was home. That did not stop us from going inside (we knew where the key was) to rest a little bit, taste some food from the fridge, and leave a thank you note before moving on.

Now they were visiting us and bringing a message. A few days before, they had been to a prayer group together with some other believers. Among different prayer requests, they had prayed for our family, even if most of the people there did not know us personally. Still, we were their brothers and sisters in Christ. One of the sisters received a message from the Lord for us. She didn't know us either, but she said the message was for the family they had prayed for. They wrote it down lest they forget it, and the Bunica family made that trip from Brașov to Bucharest, by train, just to deliver us that message.

It was about my husband and it went like this. "Vasile will be moved from one place to another, then he will be released, and shortly afterwards he will leave the country with all of his family."

I thanked them for the effort of coming all the way to Bucharest to meet us. We spent a pleasant time together, and after their departure I put the paper with the message somewhere and forgot about it.

Many believers were there for us and they supported us in prayer, but the reality blinded me. I could not understand and believe the work of God, for my "Joseph" was still in prison. The Lord had warned me through His word about it long before it happened, but I had refused to believe Him. However, His word came true and the loss was mine. Furthermore God's word said that "Joseph" was going to be released from prison and become a blessing to his brothers. My mind and my heart were not able to see so far as to understand that nothing was random and that everything worked together for good for those who loved God. I had to realize (as it happened only later) that it was not enough just to believe God's Word in general, but I needed to apply it in my personal life as well, regardless of the circumstances I faced.

Once two young missionaries who visited us testified:

> We had to take some aid to a poor family in a Communist country. While we were in our hotel room before leaving to fulfill our mission, we read Psalm 23. It says, "Goodness and mercy shall follow me." We said "Amen," thanked the Lord, and left. On the way we noticed that two people were following us and we could not see the connection between them and the goodness and mercy of God we were promised. We had to choose between believing what we saw and believing the Word of God that told us His goodness and mercy were following us. We chose to believe the Lord. We laughed together about our situation and went ahead. The Lord has blessed us indeed and made our mission a blessing as well, because we decided to live by faith.

My heart was divided between two worlds. I wanted to believe the world of God's Kingdom but my eyes were still focusing on the kingdom of this world.

You Must Die If You Want to Live

One afternoon I returned home, sad as usual. The children were with my parents and the house seemed so empty without them. I took the mail from the post box and my eyes fell on an official envelope sent by the Prison Department. My heart stopped and my knees started to shake. What could it be about? I opened the envelope with trembling hands and the words I read struck me. Vasile had been transferred from the prison of Rahova to the one in Aiud. No further explanation.

Everybody knew the latter as the prison of horror. Those who were sentenced for many years ended up there. The Secret Police agents had threatened Vasile repeatedly that his two year sentence would allow them to find out everything they wanted to know from him, and that afterwards he would be convicted for many more years. All these thoughts were swarming in my mind like a hammer hitting my brain. However, the Word of God tells us to rejoice when we face various troubles. Where had my joy vanished?

Suddenly, something as cold as death shrouded my heart and mind. Some persistent thoughts invaded me with such strength, it was as if someone was pushing them there with anger and hatred. "Don't you see that you're all alone? Can't you see you are abandoned? You trust in God and He doesn't even care. You pray, but He doesn't answer. You serve Him in vain. It's not worth it being His child. Vasile is still in prison."

I felt my soul filling with a deathly fear, as the presence of the evil one and his temptation tried to crush me.

"Get behind me, Satan!" I said.

In the agony of those moments I fell on my knees and I prayed, groaning, without uttering one word. "Father God, I am your child, saved by the blood and sacrifice of your Son, Jesus. Maybe it's true I do not deserve your love, but please don't chase me away from you. I am your child. Let me love you. I'm not asking for anything else. You can do with me or with Vasile anything you want. My only desire is to love and serve you unconditionally. Even if you do not give me anything else from now on, I just want to be your child, and I will ask for nothing else.

Please forgive me!"

I stayed there on the floor, and somehow a deep peace, a tender warmth and joy overwhelmed me. All terror, bitterness and fear were gone. I was a new person. I had found the Lord again. He was there with me. I was in his arms and I did not even want to move. My will was no longer on the throne of my heart.

There isn't room for two thrones in the human heart. There's room for only one, and we can sit there ourself and be miserable in spite of our wealth, or we can choose Jesus and then be happy no matter the circumstances.

No, the Lord had not left me—He had just made me understand that without Him there was no life, no peace and no real joy.

I felt I was now a new being. I could once again look people in the eyes and enjoy my children and God's daily provision, although my "Joseph" was still in prison. My prayers changed. I prayed that God would give Vasile strength and protection and I also asked the Lord that his will be done.

Now I knew that we would experience many miracles. I was looking at my life as if I was watching a movie, and I was curious to see what would happen.

Aiud: Prophetic Promise

I told my family of Vasile's transfer to Aiud. When Dorinel understood the situation, his face brightened and his eyes filled with joy. He said to me, "Mom, do you remember the prophecy from Brașov? Where is that paper? It said that Daddy would be soon moved from one place to another and then released. Aiud is a different place. That means Dad is coming home soon."

While traveling by train to Aiud I was thinking about our friends there, Gicu and Stela Stan. Gicu was the pastor of a church. I went to them to share the news. Vasile was in their town, but he was locked behind thick walls and bars. They received me with open hearts, and

I welcomed their promise that they would pray for him.

Vasile had a stomach condition and it was very difficult for him to get to a doctor while in prison. Stela told me that she worked at the town's hospital with a physician who was in charge with the local prison too, where he went once a week. She promised she would ask that doctor to examine Vasile and to convey his some messages from his family and from his brothers and sisters in Christ so that he would be reminded he was not forgotten in his suffering.

Pastor Gicu Stan and his wife Stela

I was glad we had that opportunity and I gave her a photo of Vasile so the doctor could recognize him. That was all I could do. But I knew that our heavenly Father was able and wanted to do more than we asked for or thought of.

Gicu and Stela insisted that I should spend the night with them and go home the next day. I thanked them but I felt the urge to go back right then with the night train. So I arrived home late that night, tired from the long journey and all the emotional turmoil I had been through.

Grandpa's Gift

Arriving home, I opened the gate of the small yard in front of our apartment house. Then in the dark I noticed a man sleeping on a chair in front of our building's entrance. As I drew near him I recognized "Grandpa", the father of Brother Tudorel from Dofteana. I touched him on the shoulder. When he saw me his face lit up, and he stood and said cheerfully, "Praise the Lord, dear Pușa. It's great you came home. I was afraid I would not meet you."

"But what happened, Grandpa? Why did you travel all the way to Bucharest?"

"Look, we've butchered a calf and I brought you some of what the Lord has given us."

How great is our God! Grandpa had come from Dofteana, and he had traveled more than I had. He had to walk to the train station and from there to my apartment, all while carrying a bag full of food for us. When he arrived at our apartment nobody was home, but he stayed at the door and waited. Then I understood why I could not spend the night in Aiud and why I insisted to return home the very same day. How could I ever forget the kindness of this brother's gesture?

The food he brought to us as a gift was more precious than diamonds. No one would suspect the brilliant beauty that can be found in a piece of rock or coal. But the fire and the pressure reveal it. How many of us hide diamonds in the clay that we are shaped of? We complain when the fires of trials and hardships come over us, but will we recognize ourselves when we are going to shine in His heavenly Kingdom? The truth is, it will be hard to recognize ourselves because we will bear the image of Him who left His glory to put on our image.

"Oh, God, please reward Grandpa for the love he has shown us!" I prayed silently.

After about two weeks I got news from Stela. The doctor had been able to see Vasile and everything went well. She could not send me the details by mail.

Vasile's Discharge

Two months had passed since my husband was moved to Aiud and I thought I would soon be allowed to go see him. Then one day I received a letter from the judge in charge of Vasile's case, in which he asked me to go see him. I did not know the reason behind his request but I thought that meeting might give me the chance to find out why they moved Vasile to Aiud.

That judge had seemed an honest man, at least compared to others. (That's how I had perceived him, but who could know if I was right?)

I was surprised that he welcomed me with a smile and graciously offered me a chair. Although very curious to see what was coming next, I decided not to ask him anything. I thought that since he was the one who called me, he should be the first to speak.

After some small talk about how the children and I were doing (How had he suddenly become so interested in our lives?), he told me why I had been summoned there. "Mrs. Răscol, I assume you'd like to have your husband home with you and see him set free."

"Do you have any doubt about this?"

"No, I don't. That is why I have a proposal for you. You donate to me the car in which the Bibles were found, and I promise your husband will be a free man. (The car he was talking about was an Opel we had received shortly before Vasile was arrested; Nelu and Neculai had parked it somewhere in a secluded place.)

For a moment I thought it was a bad joke. It would have been too much for that man to mess with my emotions. Who would have hesitated if given the chance to exchange a car for the freedom of a loved one? Certainly not me. However, I thought it could have been a trap meant to take my car, only to tell me later that he was sorry but he couldn't keep his part of the deal.

"Your Honor, do you really mean it?"

"Absolutely."

"But remember, you told me that nothing could be done in this case."

"Times and events have changed in the meantime."

"How will I know that you will keep your word?"

"Very simple. You bring the car tomorrow and I will show you the official discharge document."

"Can you give it to me personally, so that I can go with it to Aiud immediately and take Vasile home?"

"Sure, if you want I can hand the document to you instead of mailing them."

"Okay, I'll be back tomorrow. I get the discharge document and you get the car."

"OK. See you tomorrow."

I thought I was dreaming. I hurried to tell the good news to the family members and our close friends. Then I also called Gicu Stan from Aiud and Vasile's parents from Pătrăuți. I was giddy with joy.

When I had finally come to the point of being happy and content just by having the Lord, not by getting what I wanted from Him, and when the Lord became my everything, in His perfect kindness He fulfilled the desires of my heart. These desires had started to mirror His will. I was beginning to understand the meaning of the words, "You must die if you want to live," "You must give if you want to have," and "You must be blind in order to see."

The next day I raced from the courthouse to the airport with that precious document in my hand. Then I got off the plane, where the Stans were waiting for me, and rushed to the prison in Aiud. I was upset that time was passing so slowly and my legs were not moving faster.

When we arrived at the prison gate it was already late in the afternoon. I went to the clerk behind the counter, showed him the paper and asked for my husband.

"Don't be in such a hurry. Things don't happen as fast and simple as you think, he said. It's too late to do all the formalities today. Come back tomorrow."

"Tomorrow? But why? This paper has today's date written on it and this day has not ended yet. My husband is a free man starting from today. You're holding him in prison illegally until tomorrow."

"Enough of that already! Go now and come back tomorrow!" he barked at me and closed the window.

Tomorrow seemed an eternity away. I went to the Stans where I stayed overnight, but the next day, early in the morning, I was back at the prison office along with Gicu. I handed over the document and we both waited in front of the gate.

After a while I saw Vasile coming slowly, his eyes searching everything around him. When he saw us his face lit up with a smile. He was so skinny! He had never been fat, but now he was terribly skinny. "Never mind, I thought, all that matters is that he's coming home. I will make sure afterwards that he'll gain back the lost weight."

Within minutes we were all outside and I heard the gate closing—but this time behind us. Praise the Lord!

It was a tender meeting with lots of hugs and tears. Gicu wanted to know how the meeting with the doctor went and Vasile told us:

"When I found out I was going to be taken from Rahova to another prison I was told only to go pack. The prison van took me to the train station. There they put me in a railway wagon designed for animals, with bars above so we could not see anything outside. We sat down inside with other inmates, like animals. In one corner was a bucket that served as restroom and another one with drinking water. Upon entering I was given food for the trip—a piece of bread and some lard. We traveled for two days. The train moved slowly and stopped often to pick up more prisoners from other stations.

"Most of them had been caught while trying to cross the border illegally, to escape the 'communist paradise'. Some succeeded, but others were caught and sentenced to long years of imprisonment. Still others were shot in the border area.

"There were about 30 or 40 of us in that railway wagon. We had no idea where we were being taken. The guards opened the door just to squeeze some more people inside. The air was stifling hot.

"When we reached our destination two days later, we were taken from the train station to the jail. Then I realized we had arrived of all places at the infamous prison in Aiud, the one I had seen so many times when I was travelling around the country. I had seen only its exterior walls and had heard about it. Everybody knew that only the ones who had long sentences to serve were sent there. I remembered that moment the threats the Secret Police agents shouted at me during the investigation: 'We'll keep you there until you confess everything!'

"They locked me in a cell with other inmates and I understood that we would be taken outside for some kind of labor. At least that was some news I could enjoy. I was assigned to the group that made wooden boxes for the field crops.

"One day while working on the boxes, deep despair and discouragement seized me. During a break I hid behind a stack of boxes, fell on my knees and prayed fervently, "Lord, I feel so deserted and discouraged. In your mercy please give me a sign that you did not forget me—a sign of your love." Then I went back to work.

"After a while, a guard came up with a list and shouted, "Those of you who hear their names will line up at the gate!"

"I kept on working but then I heard the guard calling my name so I joined the line at the gate. I understood that we were going to the doctor though I had not asked to be seen by one. Until then, whenever I requested such an appointment because I was sick I was always told, "You rascal, now you want to see a doctor too?"

"I joined the group to be taken to the doctor, who came there once a week. That was the one day when he would examine inmates who had asked to be seen by him.

"I waited at the door along with others. The inmates entered the doctor's office one at a time and had to state their name. When it was my turn and I said my name, I was told to wait some more. I stood there until all the others were seen by the doctor. I was the last one. 'They must have brought me here by mistake,' I told myself. In the end I was received into his office.

"What's your name?" the doctor asked.

"Vasile Răscol"

"He looked at me and smiled. I could not believe my eyes—somebody in that jail was smiling at me and did not call me a scumbag.

"Being alone with me in the office the doctor continued: 'I bring you a message of encouragement from your family, from your brothers and sisters in the church of God. You need to know that you're not forgotten by them or by God, and that you are loved.'

"I could hardly believe what I'd heard! He repeated my exact words as if he had stood by me when I had said that prayer just a few hours earlier. God was so great!

"The doctor went on to say, 'Here, they've sent you some chocolate. You have to eat it now. You can't get out of here with the chocolate. I could lose my job for that.'

"I gobbled it down right away. He didn't need to tell me twice. After that he examined me and recommended some medicine. Then I left. I was a different person now. I was encouraged, in high spirits and strengthened in faith."

Gicu had tears in his eyes after hearing this story.

~ PART TEN ~
Together at Last

The Lord's Supper at Home

The same evening we flew home. I had so many questions to ask my husband. I wanted to know everything that had happened in those fourteen months and seven days, but I waited patiently for the right time. I was so happy! It seemed like I was walking on clouds. Vasile looked as if he had just woken up from his sleep. He was looking closely at everything around his, as if seeing them for the first time. In fact he did see everything in a new light after a long time. On the way home he told me:

"I knew that I would be discharged."

"Who told you the news?"

"No one, but I had two dreams. You appeared in the first one and I was showing you that I was there on the third floor of the prison. I had the second dream three days ago. I was on the same third floor where I had shown you I was locked up in the previous dream, and you took the elevator, came to me and said, 'I'm going to pay for the last three days and then I'll come back.'

"I was convinced that I would be set free. I was so sure about it that yesterday I gave all the things I had to the other inmates in the cell. When the guard came up to me and ordered me to pack, I told him that I had no luggage.

"I went down from the third floor to the first where agent Stănescu was expecting me. He tried to win me over to their side, telling me how nice they were to set me free, and that I should be grateful for it and collaborate with them. He even gave me an apple to eat. Upon leaving

I received the clothes, the watch and the wedding ring that had been taken from me when I was arrested.

Back home in Bucharest, the whole family was waiting for us with excitement, but I was sure Vasile did not want to see anyone else that day.

After he hugged the children and his relatives, Vasile invited all of us to get down on our knees and thank the Lord; after that he went to take a bath, just as my father had done when he returned from prison.

Meanwhile I prepared dinner. While we sat around the table, Grandpa served us the Lord's Supper. We were the body of Christ, the broken bread. He had suffered in us. We were the body of Christ who was now back together, with Him at His table.

Home after the time spent in the prison in Aiud

The children clung to their Daddy. Cristiana did not want to leave his arms. When Vasile wanted to go in another room, Cristiana began to cry, "Daddy, don't go on a business trip again! Don't leave me here without my daddy. Promise?"

Late that evening we got the children ready for bed. After the last search, Dorian had not wanted to sleep alone in his room, but with me and Cristiana. Of course he was not "afraid", he was a big boy now, but the terror of the Secret Police was able to harm the soul of the child. I was wondering where would Dorian choose to sleep now, after his dad had come back home. As expected, he decided to sleep in our bedroom, and for quite a long time the four of us shared the same room.

I switched off the light so we could go to sleep. We both had had a long day with a strong emotional impact. Vasile could not fall asleep, nor could I. After a while I asked him, "Why can't you sleep?"

"You know, in the prison cell the light is permanently on, day and night. You learn to sleep with the light on. The guards had to be able to see us all the time. Now that I'm home in my own bed, I feel like I forgot to sleep with the light off. Do you think I could switch it on to see if I can fall asleep?"

Many nights after that we had to sleep with the light on, even if the children were not used to it.

Holiday in Sinaia

We decided to go to a mountain resort for a few days and we found a hotel in Sinaia. Vasile needed a change of scenery and some quiet time before resuming work.

We took the kids with us and it felt like we used to, on our previous vacations. I wanted Vasile to tell me about what he'd been through, but it was still too early and too painful so I had to be patient.

Brother Viski Francisc from Oradea, wanted to see Vasile. After a couple of days he heard that we were at Sinaia, so he came to meet us there.

A strong friendship connected us with this precious brother. Richard Wurmbrand, who had been with him in prison, said about him once, "If you want to see the Lord Jesus, just look at Viski."

His life was an example to everybody during all the years he spent in prison.

Now, in Sinaia, he said to Vasile, "How are you, roomie?"

After they hugged, they started talking in a language that only they, as former inmates, understood and they eventually managed to make fun of their prison experience, laughing like two children.

Vasile was finally able to relax and feel free. Brother Viski had a great sense of humor. At one point he stopped laughing and said with a serious face, "We need to be serious. What's the point of all this fun? And to prove I'm right I'll tell you a story."

A businessman from Oradea had to go to Brașov for a very important meeting. He took the night train to Bucharest, which was going to pass through Brașov. He looked for the train conductor and asked him, "Sir, I want to get off at Brașov. It's a matter of life and death. I really need to get off there but I'm exhausted and I will certainly fall asleep as soon as the train sets in motion. Would you please be so kind and wake me up then, lest I end up in Bucharest? If you have no choice, you have my permission to throw me off the train."

"Very well, sir, I will do that," the conductor promised him.

The business man lay down to relax and fell fast asleep. After a while, he felt the train shaking and coming to a full stop. He opened his eyes, looked out the window to see where he was, and to his dismay realized that he was in Bucharest, the last stop. Terribly angry, he went to find the train conductor. He found him on the platform, talking to someone. The traveler rushed at him, punched him and said, "Didn't I ask you to wake me up in Brașov?"

People gathered around them, watching the conductor who was getting what was coming without fighting back. Someone asked him, "Hey man, why do you let him punch you like that?"

"You should have seen the punches I got from the man I pushed off at Brașov," the conductor replied.

But we need to get serious now.

We all burst into laughter. We were lighthearted now and it was easier to joke and tell such stories than to allow our emotions to choke our voices, because the wounds were still fresh.

Meanwhile Vasile's hair grew again and his cheeks were not as pale as they used to be. He didn't look like a convict anymore and he could face the world without anyone suspecting where he had come from.

When we walked into our church building on Miulești Street and the congregation saw Vasile, a cry of joy broke out and many believers stood up to see him, as if he were apostle Peter who had been delivered from prison.

He was loved by our brothers and sisters in Christ. All or most of them had kept him in their prayers. I say "most of them" because some only called themselves our brothers in Christ, while they sneaked among us to spy on us as informers of the Secret Police. They were wolves in sheep's clothing, so we called such people "Brother Wolf".

When things calmed down a little we used to sit together in the evening and I was trying to make him tell me what he went through. It wasn't easy for him, but I had my own story to tell, so we took turns and told each other about the trials we had experienced, with their pain and suffering. However, we had had our share of joy as well and the greatest of all for both of us was the fact that we had never been abandoned and alone, though sometimes it felt like it.

"Vasile, what happened after you were arrested and taken from the courtroom through the back door?"

"When the trial was over I was pushed through the door of the judge's office. Before I was carried away I saw the brothers rushing after me and your father shouting and protesting. I was quickly taken out of there. Someone had given me a bag of clothes that I held in my hand. The guards and the prison van were waiting for me at the gate of the courtyard. Everything happened so fast and unexpectedly, though somewhere deep inside of me I knew I would be sentenced to prison.

"I was handcuffed and chained next to another convict. We were taken to the Police Headquarters where some papers needed to be filled in. When we got in the yard of that institution, the man who was chained next to me, who was an epileptic, had some seizures and fell down writhing. Everyone got scared and I barely managed to convince the guards to unchain him and pour some cold water on him. Then I saw you. How did you know I was taken there?"

"I asked the judge and he told me where you were going. I wanted to bring you some food and to see you one last time, although I was heartbroken. Nothing else could be done from then on."

"Indeed. They photographed, fingerprinted me and filled in my papers as if I were a regular criminal. They took my watch and wedding ring. The lack of my wedding ring hurt me terribly. Then I was taken to the Secret Police prison in Rahova where I was incarcerated. Their agents interrogated me further, asking again and again where the Bibles were coming from, who were the other members of my underground network, and who were the foreign spies I was working with.

"I prayed all the time asking for strength not to betray my brothers. After a while, if the Secret Police agents saw they could not get any information from me, they tried another method. They put me in a cell with some so-called convicts whose job was to earn my trust and discover my weaknesses, which was not too difficult. My family was what I loved the most and the lack of my children broke my heart. When they understood that was my weakness, they moved me into another cell where I could hear children playing. I had left Cristiana home after one whole year of taking her to kindergarten and back every day.

"The onslaught of memories overwhelmed me. My heart was crying and they were watching me through the peephole; when they saw I was down, they would start interrogating me again, trying to convince me: 'You are such a fool! Don't you think of your kids and your aging parents? You could be home by this time tomorrow. Just write down a statement about everything you did and you will be free to go back to your family. If you don't cooperate with us, we have our own ways to make you talk. Your sentence will be switched from two years to a lot more.'

"But something in me made me hold my ground. It wasn't something that came from within. It was a power and a persistence that did not let me fall into their trap, a strength given to me from above when all connections with the outside world were cut off.

"For six months I lived a nightmare without knowing if it would ever end.

"All the other men in my cell were political convicts. Up to that moment I had never been involved in politics; it was then that I had the chance to see what communist politics was like – ruthless, with no shame or fear of God. I was locked in a cell with a party member, an unscrupulous activist who had forced many citizens to abandon their lands to the state. Those who'd resisted had been taken into the woods and shot. He had become part of the president's entourage. However, after a while he fell into disfavor. He had harmed many innocent people in the name of the communist ideology, but somehow he wronged his "comrades" who threw him in jail. He knew he would be killed, and death terrified him. He was afraid his life would be ended during a transfer. (He knew from his own experience that the Secret Police used that method.) He could not sleep at night because he had nightmares.

"In each cell the convicts knew what the others were there for. He had heard that I was a Christian and knew why I got there. He came to me to ask about God and if there was forgiveness for a man like him who was guilty of murder. I did my best to help him. I told him how Jesus sacrificed Himself for the sins of all mankind, and I talked to him about the thief who was saved while on the cross. He started repeating some prayers after me, and he learned a few songs. I prayed with and for him, reassuring him that Jesus could forgive him, too. He slept in the bed above mine and I could often feel it shaking from his crying. Then he was transferred and I don't know what happened to him.

The Cry Behind Prison Bars

"After I was locked for about five months in that cell, my feet were swollen from lack of activity and poor blood circulation. Especially the veins on my right leg seemed like they were about to pop and the pains were terrible. I asked permission to go see a doctor. The answer was, 'What are you talking about, you scumbag, you say you need a doctor now?'

"We were all scumbags there. However, because I was getting worse, I was finally taken to the hospital. The doctor decided to remove the swollen vein. A few days after the surgery he removed the stitches and then I was sent back to prison. Soon after that I was transferred to an ordinary prison where you were allowed to come and see me.

"It was summer and we could hardly breathe because of the tin roof that became burning hot under the scorching sun. I was not allowed to lie down in my bed. I could only sit with my feet on the floor. Because of that my wound opened and the pain became unbearable. Once, when I managed to get to the small window where the air was not so hot, I just grabbed the bars with my hands and cried inwardly, 'Lord, do not leave me. Please take me to You and let me die!'

"My condition was getting worse. I was there when they let you come to see me. After you talked to the warden, the superintendent came one morning to inspect the prison, and when he saw me he said, 'What is this guy doing here? Take him out.'

"So I was moved to a more humane place, but I was together with other sick convicts. Some of them had sexually transmitted diseases. Only God protected me from getting infected. The day I was allowed to see you, the guards took me from the cell and told me, 'You'll go to a room where you'll be able to see your children too.'

"I was so happy that I could not believe my ears, but at the same time I did not want the children to see me in that place. I was not a criminal or a scumbag, though all of us were called that in prison. My surprise was even greater when they told me I could take off my striped coat and keep only the shirt. The guards added that I was not going to see the kids from behind the bars and that I would be allowed to give them some toys. I burst into tears, no longer able to hold them back. I could hardly walk on my shaking, sick legs. I went to the restroom to wash my face and calm down. It took a little to pull myself together. You know the rest of the story."

Yes, I knew it indeed, but I wanted to know what happened after that.

Now we were all at home together. However, our life was different from the one we had lived before Vasile's arrest. I had lost my job and Vasile was trying to get one now. He went to the Agricultural Academy where he had worked before his arrest, and they were all very happy to see him. They said, "Of course you can come back to work. We need you here. We will be waiting for you on Monday morning."

On Monday morning, however, they greeted him somewhat embarrassed and said, "Vasile, we can't take you back. You've had some troubles with the Secret Police, you know. We are sorry."

He was very sad when he got home. He tried to find a job in many other places but he kept on receiving the same answer. The Secret Police agents were following him everywhere he went, making sure he noticed they were always watching him. They sent him their message indirectly too. They went to Ionel, Vasile's brother, in his workshop and started a conversation. "How is your brother Vasile doing?" (As if they didn't know . . .)

"He's looking for a job."

"Tell him to quit playing the hero. He needs to provide for his family. He could earn a living easily—he could have any job he likes if he only comes to us. We'll help him get a job."

Of course, Vasile received that message but he refused their help.

One day soon after, while he was waiting for the trolley bus, agent Stănescu accosted him with a "friendly" proposal. "Vasile, why don't you want to work with us?"

This time my husband lost his temper and started to yell at him right there, in the trolley station, with lots of people staring at them. "You'd better leave me alone! Stop approaching me with such proposals! I've already paid for what I did. If you don't like it, you can arrest me again, but in the meantime, leave me alone!"

They did not approach him from that day on, but they made sure he could not find a job. Our life was completely different from the one we were used to. I had no job either. No one would hire either of us because the watchful eyes of the Secret Police were checking everything. We didn't visit anyone because we didn't want to endanger our brothers and friends. And the fear of the Secret Police prevented our friends from coming to us as well. We were young and our situation had become even more difficult than when Vasile was imprisoned.

How did we survive? It's hard to say. We had no assistance from abroad because most missionaries stopped contacting us in order not to worsen our situation. However, we received letters of encouragement that comforted us greatly.

Vasile and I with the letters

In spite of our seemingly desperate situation, the Word of God miraculously fulfilled the verse that says. "I have been young, and now am old; yet I have not seen the righteous forsaken, nor his descendants begging bread."

Before Vasile was sent to prison we were both working and had a good income, so we had what we needed. Now, with no income, our life was more plentiful than ever. Day after day we received signs of God's love through the poorest and simplest people.

One morning someone knocked on our door. When I opened it, I saw some bags filled with food and a retired older brother who had a heart condition, gasping because of the effort of climbing all those stairs with the heavy bags in his hands. It was Brother Şendrea.

"Brother Şendrea, what are you doing here with these heavy bags in your hands?"

"Heavenly Father, he whispered a prayer with tears in his eyes, thank You for helping me get here safe and sound."

His monthly income could hardly cover his own needs. However, he'd faithfully saved some of what he had and kept it for the Lord. Though he was living in poverty, his willingness to give made us rich.

Sisters and brothers whom the world despised, though it was not worthy of them, spoiled us with the finest food they could find in our stores, after having stood for hours in line to buy it.

We were overwhelmed. Then I understood the words of the Bible, "It is better to give than to receive." For years we had had the privilege of bringing gifts to many of our brethren. Had we enjoyed it too much? I do not know. But now, when we were surviving thanks to other people's gifts, we allowed others to feel the same joy. However it was not easy—not easy at all. In fact, that was the most difficult period of our lives.

Sister Suzana

One day we were visited by a sister from Heria, a Transylvanian village. It was Suzana, the sister of Nelu Man's mother. She did not come empty-handed either, but the main purpose of her visit was to tell us about an extraordinary experience she had had.

One day this summer, I was in the kitchen cooking something on the stove. I suddenly felt an urge, something like a voice that said to me, "Go and pray for Vasile." I thought I would first finish cooking and then go pray, but the Lord told me, "Leave everything and go right now." That exhortation was like an order. I left everything behind and got down on my knees to pray. While I was interceding I saw you, Vasile. Your face was tormented by suffering. You looked so bad that I got scared. You were holding the bars of the cell with your hands while crying to God. The Spirit of the Lord asked me, "Do you like how he looks?"

"Oh, God, he looks awful!"

"Go and announce a fast for him."

And so I did. Our congregation fasted for you according to God's command. It was a long, hot summer day. Now I've come to ask you what happened that day.

With tears in his eyes, Vasile told her what had happened to him back then. Everything was exactly as in our sister's vision. After that terrible day he was moved in a different cell.

Then I understood why I had found such great favor in the eyes of the prison warden. The secret was the fasting and prayers of our brothers and sisters.

After a while I remembered about the first food parcel I was allowed to take him in prison. I had put in some pieces of cheese, each wrapped separately. At home I had carefully opened the wrapper of those pieces and drew the faces of our kids (that I had cut from some photos of them) in the soft cheese. I had put the wrapper back and placed those pieces of cheese among the others. No one could have noticed that the wrapper had been opened.

"'I thought you would find them when you ate those pieces of cheese and that you would be glad to see the pictures of our children. Do you remember if you found something in there?'

Vasile looked at me with a smile and said, "I did not touch any of the food in that parcel. At that time I was sharing a cell with another believer who was being sent to the "restrictive" cell where he wouldn't get any food at all, so I gave my parcel to him. If he found the photo of the children I'm sure he prayed for them. I don't know what happened to him afterwards; I didn't see him again."

Emigration Documents

After trying in vain to get a job, Vasile decided to apply for an emigration visa. The fact that we could not earn money to cover the needs of our family was a real burden for us. We were ashamed of the people around us, but God knew our situation.

The idea of leaving the country and settling in the United States was suggested to us by the ministry directed by Brother Richard. We also remembered the message God had sent us from Brașov. "Vasile will be moved from one prison to another, then he will be released and will leave the country." The first two parts had been fulfilled and we believed the last part would come true as well.

When applying for immigration to the United States we needed to be sponsored by a family who would commit to support us. The Romanian Baptist Church in Los Angeles led by Pastor Peter Popovici sent us the warranty form. Brother Peter Popovici was a good friend of Brother Richard. Many other believers had gone to the United States before us.

The Romanian Government had adopted a new strategy. If they could not convince someone to work with them, they got rid of them by allowing them to leave the country. (Later on we found out the Romanian authorities sent their own people to keep on watching the activities of those who were allowed to immigrate.)

Among the "rebellious" ones who left Romania was the family of pastor Pânzaru. Their daughter, Cornelia, had married Neculai, Vasile's brother. After they got married, they emigrated too.

Then Victor Răscol and his family left as well. All of them promised they would do their best to help us, through the Romanian Embassy in the USA. We did not doubt their good intentions, but our hope was in God.

We kept on receiving letters of encouragement from the United States. The collaborators of Bill Batham's and Richard Wurmbrand's ministries were a source of support and encouragement for us.

As expected, our emigration request was rejected. No victory comes without a fight, so we started fighting that battle on our knees. Every week we had a special day of fasting and prayer for this purpose. Brother Vasile Șandor and Sister Maria Lazăr joined our prayers. For a year and a half, we brought this cause together before the Lord.

Meanwhile we had asked for an audience with the American Embassy in Bucharest. We wanted to know if we could get a US visa. To our surprise, they knew our situation better than we did. There we heard some amazing things. The ambassador showed us copies of newspaper articles about all the interventions that had been made abroad for Vasile's release. There had been lots of demonstrations in front of the Romanian embassies, requesting the release of the man convicted for distributing Bibles.

The climax of all that support movement had been the visit of US President Gerald Ford in Bucharest. One of the topics he discussed with President Ceaușescu was the release of my husband. (Then I understood why Neculai and I were detained at the Secret Police office without being interrogated the day President Ford came. The authorities wanted to be sure we would not try to use that opportunity to do something.)

Then I also understood the reason the judge offered so "kindly" to release Vasile in exchange for our car. The release had been obtained, but the Secret Police wanted to take our car too. Our visit to the American Embassy encouraged us during the year and a half waiting period.

The Secret Police agents had relaxed the scrutiny they had subjected us to. We had more freedom of movement and resumed contact with the free world again.

Meanwhile a group of believers wrote a petition for the Free Europe Radio Station. The document had to get there for broadcasting. It reported the many persecutions of the Secret Police against the Christian believers. Vasile had a good opportunity and sent the document abroad. It reached its destination and was read on the radio. The Secret Police were alerted, not knowing how the document got on air, and many believers were interrogated afterwards.

One day, when we were praying for our departure, Sister Maria Lazăr told us, "Children, the Lord showed me that you will leave. I saw you taking off on a plane. The time for you to go is coming soon."

However, we had just received an official letter from the Department of Emigration, in which we were told once again that our request was rejected. The news made us sad, but we knew we would eventually leave. So a few days later we filled out another application form.

The next day the phone rang and Vasile was invited to the Passport Department. We wondered why.

Once he got there he was told our application was approved. "Fill in the necessary papers, hand over all the required belongings, and then come back to receive your passports."

For us, the word passport was the equivalent of the key that would unlock the door of our prison and allow us to escape and enjoy freedom. Vasile did not ask why our request had been denied just a few days before.

He rushed back home to bring us the long-awaited news. It was in February 1977. The following days were quite busy. We had to take care of all the required formalities. We applied for a United States visa. We were told that we needed an entry visa to Italy, where we were to receive the American visa. The Italian Embassy informed us that the whole process was going to take several weeks.

Earthquake!

One evening, Vasile said to me, "We are leaving the country and my heart is filled with sadness. I wish I had the opportunity—just one more time—to help our brothers and sisters like I used to."

His words were like a prayer that rose to heaven. A few days later we were going to have a baptism service in our apartment; of course it was going to be held in secret. Brother Bratu Tudorel had asked to be baptized and he wanted the event to take place in our home.

We invited Brother Caraman to baptize him and Brother Ioanid to be present as a friend. The baptism was to be done in our bathroom (where we had secretly had many more).

While I was warming the water, we sat around the table talking about the baptism. Dorian and Cristiana were in the other room.

Suddenly the floor under my feet began shaking. I jumped from the table, realizing it was an earthquake. Vasile took the kids by the hands. They had come out of their room, scared, and he ran with them downstairs, bumping into the walls that were shaking from the fury of the earthquake.

We ran into the street. People came out of their houses and apartments, and stood frightened in the street. It was late at night and the scenery was gloomy. Cristiana was six. She started going from one person to another saying, "It's so good to have Jesus! Only He can protect us. Believe in the Lord Jesus!"

When the shaking was over, we took brothers Caraman and Ioanid home. The whole town was dark since the power lines were down. The downtown looked as if it had been bombed. Ten-story buildings had collapsed on the ground like matchboxes. The terrified people started remembering God.

The building Brother Ioanid lived in was still standing. In the darkness that covered everything he started shouting: "Leanaaaa . . ." Costeeeel . . ." And as an echo he heard their answers. Both were OK, thank God!

We left him there and ran to check on my parents. Everything was fine with them too. We left the kids with them and took Brother Caraman home; then we took Brother Tudorel to Dofteana. Trains were stuck in the train stations and he had decided to walk all the way home if he had to. He was very worried about his family.

We traveled all night. When we got to Dofteana we found out the earthquake had not been felt there at all. Then we returned back home.

The earthquake had caused huge damages, including the loss of human lives and property. The borders were opened up for the foreign aid agencies that wanted to help.

It was March 1977. And the aid started flowing. Our brothers and sisters from the free countries took action immediately. They came one after another to our door, bringing everything they thought we might need.

Our apartment had turned into a waiting room. One group was with me in one of our rooms, another one was waiting in the kitchen, while Vasile was with some other brothers in our larger room, and Dorinel with another one in the street.

We distributed humanitarian aid for days. The Secret Police had its own problems to take care of so they didn't care about us.

This is how we concluded the last chapter of our activity in Romania, activity that had been given to us and guided by the Lord.

After a few weeks, life was beginning to return to normal, but the process was not easy. Thousands of lives had been lost in that tragedy and people began to seek God more.

Meanwhile, the petition Vasile sent to Free Europe Radio Station was broadcast and triggered an intensive interrogation. The believers suspected by the Secret Police were summoned and questioned. The most important question was who had sent the document to that radio station. If the authorities found out Vasile himself was responsible for that, there's no way they would have allowed us to leave the country. The brothers who were interrogated stood strong for a while but they warned us seriously, "Do something and go. We don't know how much longer we can hold on!"

It was easy for them to tell us to leave, but the process of getting the visa was slow and we could not leave without it. Then we remembered the word of the Lord, that promised us we would eventually go.

Transit Visas

In his attempts to accelerate the process, Vasile met a friend who suggested we should go to the French Embassy and ask for a transit visa. It was issued immediately and though it was valid for three days only, it was enough for us to leave Romania. Thus we could have helped out our brothers because once we were gone they would have been able to blame Vasile for sending the petition to Free Europe Radio Station.

The French Embassy gave us a transit visa and the Swiss Embassy gave us one as well for other seven days. We were hoping to get the Italian visa in the meantime. Aunt Alice was living in Paris. She had emigrated seven years before and now she was waiting for us.

After a farewell meal, we said good bye to our loved ones.

With four suitcases and no money at all, Vasile, I and our two children were heading to the unknown. But in fact our whole life is a big unknown—each day is. Places may be familiar, but not the events of each day. However, we were guided in our journey by Someone well-known. His name is 'Wonderful, Lord of lords and King of kings.'

Farewell at the airport April 30, 1977

I remembered the dreams I had as a teen, dreams that seemed impossible at that time. I had wished I would live with my husband in an apartment that would have a bathroom and hot water; I also dreamed of a car and the chance to travel with my husband and see the world.

Now our flight to Paris was fulfilling the last of them. I felt the good and smiling eyes of the Lord watching over us while saying: "Seek first My kingdom and My righteousness, and all these things shall be added unto you" (Matthew 6:33).

It was time to leave the past behind and turn our eyes to the future that lay ahead, which of course was known by our Lord.

I looked at our children. They were so anxious to get to Paris and meet Aunt Alice. Vasile also seemed contaminated by their exuberance. I joined them and I wondered if any of us will remember some French once we arrived in Paris.

The question became very important once we landed in Orly Airport in Paris, where we got completely lost. Waves of people were heading in all directions; the lights and billboards, the signs with different meanings made us lose any sense of orientation.

Which way is the exit? we wondered. It was an important question. Our French proved quite poor so we had to leave aside our claims of French speaking people and ask Dorian to save us with his German knowledge.

Our Paris Refuge

And so, after quite a long time, we finally arrived at the exit where Aunt Alice was waiting for us overly worried.

"What happened to you?" she asked with a smile of relief. "I was afraid something happened and you were not allowed to leave Romania after all."

We wished we could give her an honorable explanation, but we had to admit, somewhat embarrassed, that we got lost while looking for our luggage.

Our reunion brought tears of joy, hugs and kisses.

"Dorinel, did you miss me?" Aunt Alice asked our son.

"Yes, Aunt Alice, very much."

"Me too," said Cristiana, eager to get the same attention. (She was born after the departure of Aunt Alice.)

Our taxi drive seemed like a real adventure to us. We did not know where to focus our attention – at the high speed of the car that drove so fast through the city or at the places we passed by, about which we could only dream of until then.

Aunt Alice told us more details about the ministry Brother Richard Wurmbrand was leading, which had representatives in many countries.

The three-day transit visa we had expired so quickly. It was now time to continue our journey to Switzerland, where we could stay for one week. Waving goodbye to Aunt Alice, this time we parted with a joyful heart. The Iron Curtain was not separating us anymore. We could meet again anytime.

We took the train from Paris to Bern. Heidi Fluri and Hans Zürcher, both involved in the Christian ministry in Switzerland, were waiting for us at the train station. Heidi had come several times in Romania, to bring aids for the persecuted believers, and that's how we got to know her. We were glad to see someone we knew in that foreign country.

Our friends took us to a hotel in Thun where we had a dreamlike panorama. In fact, the whole trip was like a dream. It was so beautiful it didn't seem real. Our only concern during the seven day period we were allowed to stay in Switzerland was regarding the visa for Italy. What if we did not get the visa in time? There was nowhere else we could go. But we could not allow worry to overwhelm us. The One who had cared for us all along was certainly going to do it till the end. All we needed was faith.

On the morning of May 4, 1977, Brother Hans took us out for breakfast. While we were sitting around the table he handed us a small size Bible with a dedication written on its first page. It was in fact a message from God he had received for us—a Bible verse from Genesis 24:7: "The Lord God of heaven, who took me from my father's house and from the land of my birth, and who spoke to me and who swore to me, saying, 'To your descendants I will give this land,' He will send His angel before you..."

Five days later we were traveling by train to Rome, with the Italian visa in our passports and with a greater confidence in the Lord who had promised to be with us until... THE END.

Appendix 1

Petition to the Government of Romania

The parties to his petition consider themselves bound by their conscience to petition you, sir, in a matter concerning them most profoundly, thus hoping it will be solved humanely and democratically, in the spirit of justice.

We are Neo-Protestant believers, belonging to one or the other of the fourteen State-recognized denominations, whose unrestricted activity is ensured by law, as repeatedly confirmed by the President of our country. The very phase "unrestricted activity" has been taken by us from one of your speeches, sir. We would like to point out the speech given on May 23, 1974, on the occasion of opening the Congress of the Front of Socialist Unity by our country's President, Comrade Nicolae Ceaușescu, in which the statement reiterated by his excellence has been greatly welcomed by the our country's believers.

In fact, the right to practice freely one's own religion is enshrined in the basic law of our land, and in the Constitution, being in agreement with the international guaranties pledged by Romania. Thus the "Universal Declaration of Human Rights" adopted by the United Nations on December 10, 1948, expressly guarantees everyone's right to manifest his or her religion in teaching, practice, worship and observance (Article 18), as well as "the right to freedom of opinion and expression… [the] freedom to hold opinions without interference and to seek, receive and impart information and ideas through any media and regardless of frontiers" (Article 19).

However, by the issuance of Law No. 3 of 1974, duly published in the Official Monitor Nr. 48 of April 1, 1974, a situation was created which calls into question, and, in fact, nullifies our right to religious information, thus negating our right to practice our religion.

This is made clear to us by the case in which Comrade Vasile Răscol of Bucharest, Dr. Mirinescu Street nr. 12, finds himself. He has been charged with having received from abroad and distributed throughout the country Bibles and other religious books printed in Romanian. The case is due to be tried by the Court of District 6 of the City of Bucharest this year on July 23 (case Nr. 4152).

Some time ago one hundred thousand Bibles were published in our country; however, we had no access to these, since they were made available exclusively to the Orthodox believers. This discrimination applies also to the fact that the Orthodox denomination is allowed to print a number of theological books, while the Neo-Protestant denominations enjoy no such rights.

This is why, for our spiritual nourishment, both through the Bible, as well as through other religious literature, we have to depend exclusively on what is being printed for us abroad. In this context, we have to mention that of all the literature printed for us abroad, the parties to this petition are not aware of any book containing ideas subversive to our State or to the Socialist Order.

Thus for a number of years we have been receiving Bibles and other religious books printed abroad through the post or through foreign citizens, with the recipients passing them on. We understand that in this process of receiving and distributing Bibles and other religious literature many citizens of our country are involved. Until recently, there was no such law stopping us from doing this; however, we understand from the way in which articles 90 and 94 of the Press Law are being applied to Vasile Răscol that something we did freely has suddenly become a crime, and that, from now on, thousands of believers in our country are considered potential breakers of the law. For which of us, upon having a visitor bring Bibles, will turn them down, and refuse to pass them along to people who beg for Bibles from us?

So we understand that the trial of Vasile Răscol for Bible distribution is placing us all under such accusation—thousands of people in our country are now likely to be put on trial. We are convinced that these thousands of believers will not cease to receive and distribute Bibles, and other religious books, for this is an obligation of their conscience. And our being forced to get them from abroad is due to our inability to produce them in our own country. So, by quoting anew the Universal Declaration of Human Rights, it is our right to "seek, receive and impart information and ideas through any media and regardless of frontiers" (Article 19).

The signatories of this petition are of the opinion that today, while Romania is increasingly involved internationally, and the free circulation of ideas becomes dearer to people everywhere, a banning of the Bible and of religious literature, as stipulated in Articles 90 and 94 of the Press Law, would gravely harm the prestige of our country.

This would also be a denial of the religious freedom of several millions of our country's citizens.

Therefore, we plead with you, sir, to consider stopping the trial proceedings against Vasile Răscol.

However, should this trial continue on the docket, we respectfully ask that you consider us, too, as chargeable along with Vasile Răscol, thus honoring us by placing us among the accused, for spreading the Word of God.

Popescu Aurelian	Șos. Mihai Bravu 107
Diac Viorel	Bdul. Metalurgiei 42
Caraman C-tin	Cal. 13 Septembrie 38
Boeru Gheorghe	Str. Poteraș 31
Danciu Nicolae	Str. Puțul cu Tei 20
Ionescu Aurel	Str. Viilor 95
Cafengiu Aurel	Str. Ardealului 11
Nicolescu Pavel	Str. Vlad Județul 35
Nicola Ioan	Str. Diligenței 22

Tovarășe Ministru,

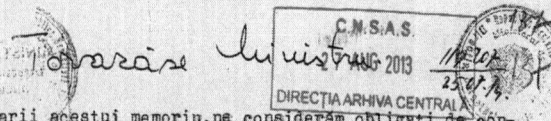

Semnatarii acestui memoriu, ne considerăm obligați de conștiința noastră, să ne adresăm Dumneavoastră într-o problemă care ne afectează profund, sperînd că vom obține pe această cale, o rezolvare umană și democratică în spiritul dreptății.

Sîntem credincioși neo-protestanți, făcînd parte dintr-unul din cele 14 culte recunoscute de Stat, a căror activitate nestînjenită este asigurată prin lege, și confirmată în repetate rînduri, de Președintele Statului nostru. Insăși expresia "activitate nestînjenită" o luăm dintr-unul din discursurile Domniei Sale. Ținem să arătăm că discursul ținut în 23 mai ac. la deschiderea Congresului Frontului Unității Socialiste de către Conducătorul Statului, Tovarășul Nicolae Ceaușescu, în care Domnia Sa a afirmat din nou în mod răspicat și limpede dreptul cetățenesc de a practica o credință religioasă, a fost salutat cu deosebită bucurie, de milioanele de credincioși din țara noastră.

Dreptul de exercitare liberă a cultului, este de altfel prevăzut în Legea fundamentală a țării, în Constituție și el este în conformitate cu angajamentele internaționale ale României. Astfel, în Declarația Universală a drepturilor Omului, adoptată de către Adunarea Generală a O.N.U. în 10 dec. 1948, se prevede în mod expres libertatea oricărui om de a-și manifesta religia prin învățătură, practici religioase, cult și îndeplinirea ritualurilor (art.18) precum și dreptul, și libertatea de a căuta, de a primi, și de a răspîndi informații și idei prin orice mijloace, independent de frontierele de Stat (art.19)

Ori noi nu avem cunoștință că România, și-ar fi retras adeziunea de la această Declarație Universală a Drepturilor Omului.

Iată însă, că odată cu apariția Legii nr.3/1974, publicată în Buletinul Oficial nr.48 din 1 IV 1974, s-a creeat o situație care pune sub semnul întrebării și care în fapt, tinde să reducă la zero, dreptul nostru de informare religioasă și prin aceasta, dreptul nostru de a ne practica credința.

Faptul acestax devine clar, din situația în care se află tov. Rascol Vasile din București str. Dr. Marinescu nr.12. Dînsul este pus sub acuzație, pentrucă a primit din străinătate și a difuzat în țară Biblii și alte cărți religioase tipărite în limba romînă.

Procesul urmează să se judece la Tribunalul Sectorului 6 al Municipiului București, în 24 iulie a.c. (Dosar nr.4152)

Se știe credem, ce înseamnă Biblia pentru noi creștinii.

Dreptul de a o obține, de a o poseda, de a o citi și de a o răspîndi, este pentru noi, tot una cu dreptul de a ne practica religia.

2.

Cu cîțiva ani în urmă,s-au tipărit în țara noastră 1oo.ooo de Biblii,dar acestea nu ne-au fost accesibile nouă,ci doar credincioșilor Ortodoxi.Discriminarea aceasta,se extinde și la faptul că cultul Ortodox,își poate tipări un oarecare număr de f cărți teologice,pe cînd cultele neoprotestante,nu au dreptul să facă nici un fel de astfel de tipărituri.

Iată dece pentru hrănirea noastră spirituală,atît prin Biblii, cît și prin altă literatură religioasă,noi sîntem obligați să depindem totalmente de ceea ce se tipărește pentru noi peste hotare.

Aici trebue să facem precizarea că,din toată literatura care se tipărește pentru noi în străinătate,semnatarii acestui memoriu, nu cunosc nici o carte care să conțină idei împotriva Statului nostru,sau a orînduirii Socialiste.

De ani de zile,noi primim deci Biblii și alte cărți religioase tipărite în străinătate,prin poștă sau prin turiști streini și cei care le primesc,le difuzează și altora.Noi apreciem,că în acest proces de primire și de răspîndire a Bibliei,și literaturii religioase,se află angrenați mii și mii de cetățeni ai patriei noastre.

Pînă în prezent,nu exista nici o lege care să ne oprească de a face acest lucru.Iată însă că în felul în care i se aplică lui Răscol Vasile articolele 9o și 94 din Legea presei,înțelegem că în ceea ce făceam pînă acum în mod liber,a devenit un delict și că de acum înainte,mii de credincioși din țara noastră,sînt puși în ilegalitate,căci care dintre noi,dacă va veni un vizitator și-i va aduce cîteva Biblii,se va abține să nu le primească și să nu le dea mai departe,atîtor oameni care ne solicită Biblii?

Înțelegem deci,că procesul intentat lui Răscol Vasile,pentru difuzarea de Biblii,ne pune pe toți sub acuzare,și dintr-odată,mii de oameni din țara noastră,se pot aștepta la asemenea procese.

Noi sîntem convinși,că acești mii de credincioși,nu se vor opri de a primi și răspîndi Biblii,și alte cărți religioase,deoarece, aceasta este o datorie a vieții noastre religioase,și o obligație de conștiință.Iar faptul că sîntem obligați să le primim din străinătate,se datorește imposibilității în care ne aflăm de a le produce în țara noastră.Ori,referindu-ne din nou la"Declarația drepturilor omului",este un drept al nostru "de a căuta,de a primi și de a răspîndi informații și idei,prin orice mijloace și independent de frontierele de Stat"(art.19)

Semnatarii acestui memoriu,consideră că astăzi cînd România se angrenează tot mai intens în viața mondială și cînd libera circulație a ideilor devine o idee tot mai scumpă oamenilor de pretutindeni, a încadra Biblia și literatura religioasă în articolele 9o și 94 din

3.

Legea Presei, ar aduce enorme deserviții numelui bun al țării noastre. Deasemenea, faptul acesta, ar fi o negare a libertății religioase a cîtorva milioane de cetățeni ai Patriei noastre.

Vă rugăm deci, să luați în considerare problema aceasta, și să sistați procesul intentat lui Răscol Vasile.

Dacă însă procesul acesta va rămîne pe rol, vă rugăm să ne puneți sub acuzare ca și pe Răscol Vasile, pentru a ne da ceea ce noi considerăm onoarea de a sta alături de el pe banca acuzaților.

Numele și pronumele	Adresa	Semnătura

Numele și prenumele	Adresa	Semnătura
Popescu Aurelian	Șos. Mihai Bravu 107	
Diac Viorel	Bdul. Metalurgei 42	
Caraman	Cal. 13 Septembrie 38	
Boeru Gheorghe	Str. Foteraș 31	
Danciu Nicolae	Str. Țutulea Toi 20	
Ionescu Aurel	Șos. Viilor 95	
Cafengiu Aurel	Str. Ardealului 11	
Nicolescu Pavel	Str. Vlad Județul 35	
Nicola Ioan	Str. Diligenței 22	

Appendix 2

Letters of Encouragement

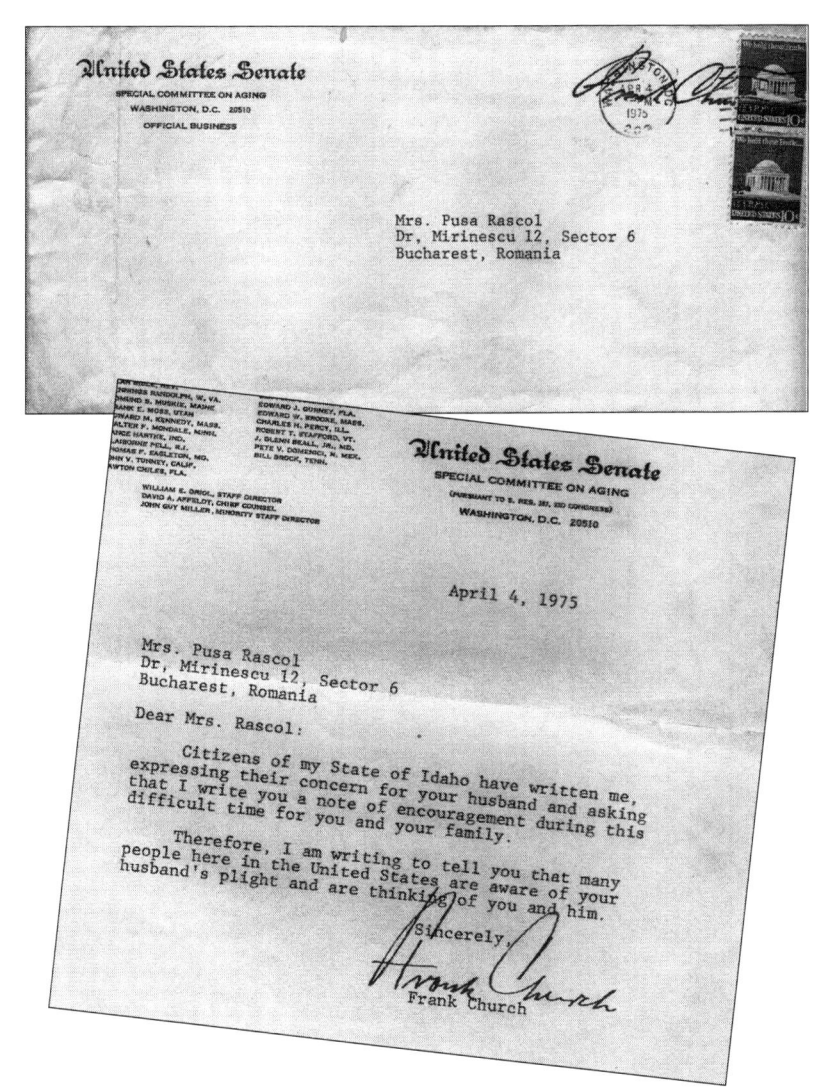

> United States Senate
> SPECIAL COMMITTEE ON AGING
> WASHINGTON, D.C. 20510
> OFFICIAL BUSINESS
>
> Mrs. Pusa Rascol
> Dr, Mirinescu 12, Sector 6
> Bucharest, Romania

> United States Senate
> SPECIAL COMMITTEE ON AGING
> (PURSUANT TO S. RES. 20, 93D CONGRESS)
> WASHINGTON, D.C. 20510
>
> April 4, 1975
>
> Mrs. Pusa Rascol
> Dr, Mirinescu 12, Sector 6
> Bucharest, Romania
>
> Dear Mrs. Rascol:
>
> Citizens of my State of Idaho have written me, expressing their concern for your husband and asking that I write you a note of encouragement during this difficult time for you and your family.
>
> Therefore, I am writing to tell you that many people here in the United States are aware of your husband's plight and are thinking of you and him.
>
> Sincerely,
>
> Frank Church

214   FLIGHT TO FREEDOM

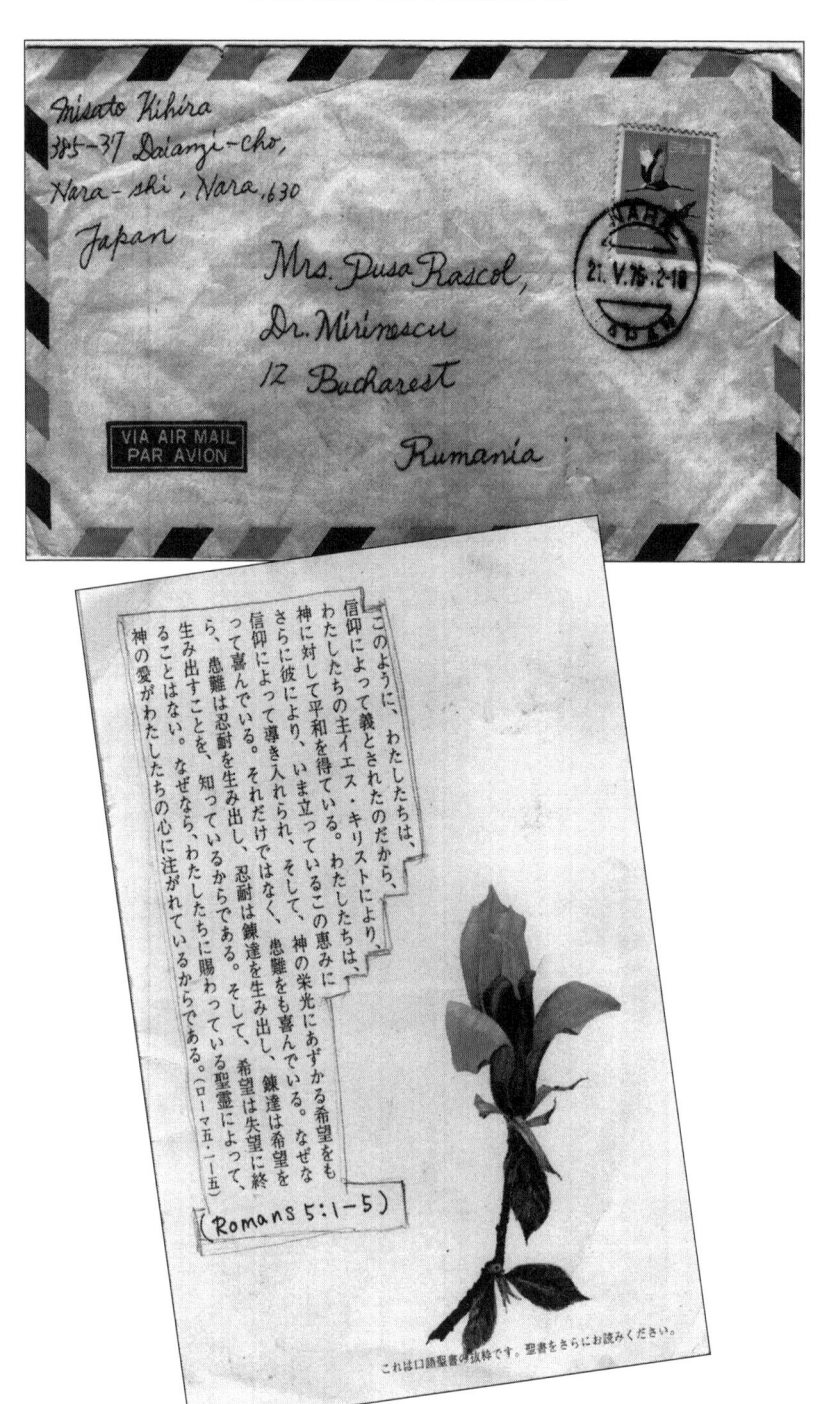

このように、わたしたちは、信仰によって義とされたのだから、わたしたちの主イエス・キリストにより、神に対して平和を得ている。わたしたちは、さらに彼によって導き入れられ、いま立っているこの恵みに信仰によって喜んでいる。それだけではなく、患難をも喜んでいる。なぜなら、患難は忍耐を生み出し、忍耐は錬達を生み出し、錬達は希望を生み出すことを、知っているからである。そして、希望は失望に終ることはない。なぜなら、わたしたちに賜わっている聖霊によって、神の愛がわたしたちの心に注がれているからである。(ローマ五・一-五)

(Romans 5:1-5)

これは口語聖書の抜粋です。聖書をさらにお読みください。

God's Faithfulness in Communist Romania   215

FLIGHT TO FREEDOM

Envelope:

Air Mail

Pusa Rascol,
Str. Dr. Mirinescu 12,
BUCHAREST,
Romania.

Letter:

Anne Halliwell,
20, Parklands Court
Great West Road
Hounslow West,
Middx. TW5 9AU
Gt Britain.

1st July, 1975.

Dear Pusa and family
 Greetings in the name of our Doamne Isuse!
 We want to assure you that we shall
Rugați-vă neîncetat for you and your family.
 Until we all are able to join together with our
Doamne Isuse in heaven, we greet you with the words, Dacă sînteți
batjocoriți pentru Numele lui Hristos, ferice de voi! Fiindcă Duhul
slavei, Duhul lui Dumnezeu, Se odihnește peste voi.
 Orice lucru veți cere, când vă rugați, să credeți că
l-ați și primit, si-l veți avea.
 și astfel vom fi totdeauna cu Domnul!
 Doamne Isuse bless you!

 Anne +

God's Faithfulness in Communist Romania

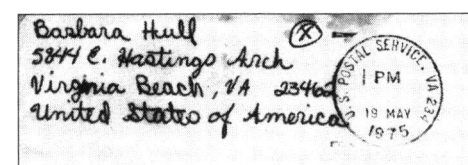

Barbara Hull
5844 E. Hastings Arch
Virginia Beach, VA 23464
United States of America

AIR MAIL

Mrs. Rusa Rascol
Dr. Mirinescu 12
Sector 6
Bucharest, Romania

May 18, 1975

Dear Rusa Rascol,

Pace Domnului to you Sister and to your children! I am a Christian in the state of Virginia of the United States of America and I have heard what has happened to your husband, Vasile. I am praying for your husband and you and your two children each day. The circumstances leading to your husband's imprisonment are being told to other Christians in The United States. I am asking them to pray for your husband and family and to write to the Romanian Embassy in The United States on behalf of your husband. Remember Rusa that nothing is impossible with God!

The apostle Paul writes to the Christians in Rome

```
HAROLD L. GURSKE
    ATTORNEY AT LAW
   205 SLOCUM BLDG.
  FALLS CITY, NEBRASKA
```

September 17, 1974

Mrs. Prusa Rascol
Dr. Mirinescu 12
Sector 6
Bucharest, Romania

Pace Domnului,

Permit me as a Christian to extend my sincere sympathy to you in the ordeal that you are experiencing because your husband, Vasile Rascol, passed out Bibles to be distributed in Romania.

I am sure you remember that the Apostle Paul and Silas were cast into prison for carrying the message of Christianity, and this is exactly what has happened to your husband.

The Christian people in America are praying for your husband's release and I am sure you are aware that the Bible tells us "Pray ye one for another." I sincerely hope that your husband will soon be released to return to his family.

Yours truly,

Harold L. Gurske
Attorney at Law

God's Faithfulness in Communist Romania

Ribeirão Preto (Brasil), 18 de outubro de 1975.

Querido irmão em Cristo
Vasile Rascol:

I'll write this letter in English, although our language is Portuguese, for I know it will be easily understood.

I read about you in a newspaper that speaks about the sufferings of our brothers and sisters who live behind the Iron Courtain.

Brother, we are with you. We are praying for you. Our church here is praying for you. Believe in our Lord. He said: "In the world ye shall have tribulation; but be of good cheer; I have overcome the world" (John 16:33).

In a very short time, according to His Word "The kingdoms of this world are become the kingdoms of our Lord and of His Christ; and He shall reign for ever and ever" (Revelation 11:15). Then we will be governed by Him, as to say, by a just government. And, more than this, we will have "power over the nations" and we'll sit with Him in His throne". (Revelation 3:21 and 2:26). Halellujah!

Rejoice, brother, for this time is at hand! Not many years shall pass, before He comes!

If you are able, please, send me an answer. If you can't, anyway, I'll pray for you with my church. May the Lord strenghten you all.

In Christ, as a member of the same Body,

Adiel A. Oliveira

Address: Rua João Clapp, 1110
14100 - RIBEIRÃO PRETO - SP
BRASIL

MARK LANE
HHC 1ST BN 6TH INF.
APO N.Y. 09140

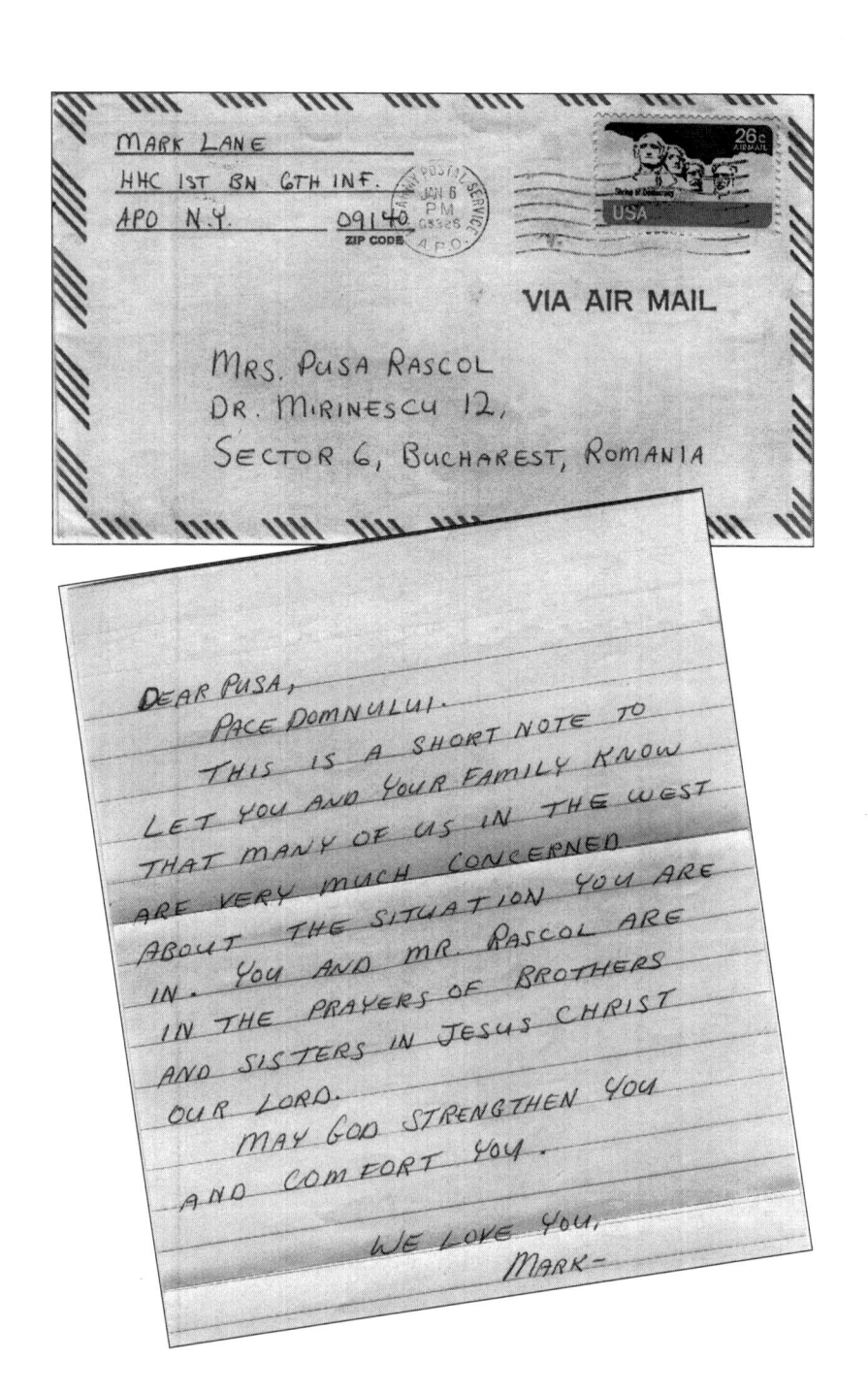

MRS. PUSA RASCOL
DR. MIRINESCU 12,
SECTOR 6, BUCHAREST, ROMANIA

VIA AIR MAIL

DEAR PUSA,
PACE DOMNULUI.
THIS IS A SHORT NOTE TO LET YOU AND YOUR FAMILY KNOW THAT MANY OF US IN THE WEST ARE VERY MUCH CONCERNED ABOUT THE SITUATION YOU ARE IN. YOU AND MR. RASCOL ARE IN THE PRAYERS OF BROTHERS AND SISTERS IN JESUS CHRIST OUR LORD.
MAY GOD STRENGTHEN YOU AND COMFORT YOU.
WE LOVE YOU,
MARK

God's Faithfulness in Communist Romania

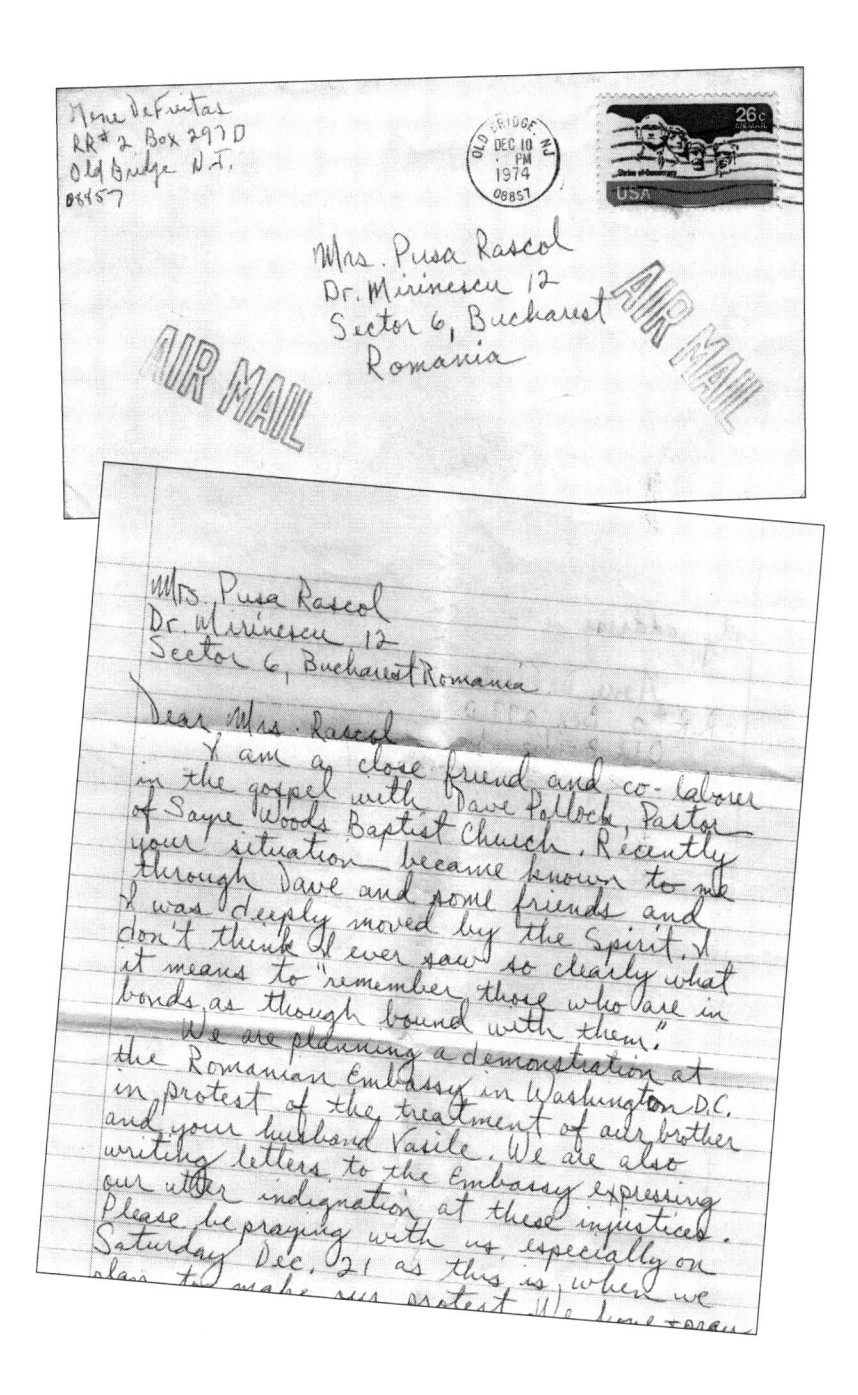

Irene DeFreitas
RR #2 Box 297D
Old Bridge, N.J.
08857

Mrs. Pusa Rascol
Dr. Mirinescu 12
Sector 6, Bucharest
Romania

AIR MAIL

Mrs. Pusa Rascol
Dr. Mirinescu 12
Sector 6, Bucharest Romania

Dear Mrs. Rascol,

I am a close friend and co-labour in the gospel with Dave Pollock, Pastor of Sayre Woods Baptist Church. Recently your situation became known to me through Dave and some friends and I was deeply moved by the Spirit. I don't think I ever saw so clearly what it means to "remember those who are in bonds, as though bound with them."

We are planning a demonstration at the Romanian Embassy in Washington D.C. in protest of the treatment of our brother and your husband Vasile. We are also writing letters to the Embassy expressing our utter indignation at these injustices. Please be praying with us especially on Saturday Dec. 21 as this is when we plan to make our protest.

Vasile Rascol
Jilava-Gefängnis
Rumänien

Erich Märker
5276) Oberwiehl
Dornbuschstraße 2

Liebe Brüder im Herrn Jesus Christus, Vasile!

In der Liebe Jesu sorgen wir uns – und viele andere mit uns – um Dich.
Wir – und viele andere – beten für Dich zu unserm Herrn und Heiland Jesus Christus.
Wir beten für Deine Familie, für Deine Gemeinde und für Dein Land, für alle Christen in der Verfolgung und für Eure Verfolger, denn Jesus Christus will auch sie in Seiner Liebe zu Menschen der Liebe Gottes machen.
Er hat alles für uns getan.

In der Liebe Jesu verbunden.
Der Friede des Herrn sei mit Dir!

Dein Bruder in Christus

Erich Märker
Reinhold Grimmer
Karl Heinbach
Helmut Gilhausen
Margitta Gilhausen

Mit uns grüßen Dich
Artur Märker
Irmtraut Märker

422 So. 5th St.
Minneapolis, Minn.
U.S.A. 55415

Mrs. Pusa Rascol
Dr. Mirinescu 12
Sector 6, Romania
Bucharest, Romania

Dear Mrs. Rascol:
The trial and imprisonment of your beloved husband has come to my attention. My wife and I hold you in our prayers.
I am the president emeritus of the American Lutheran Church.
Yours in Christ,
Fredrik

Mrs. Pusa Rascol
Dr. Mirinescu 12
Sector 6, Bucharest
Romania

May Vasile be restored to you soon! The circumstances of his arrest are known and we are not silent.

We shall meet in our Nation.

Sincerely
Dena Boswell

```
210 N. Indiana Ave.
Griffith, Ind.  46319
United States of America
```

air Mail

```
Mrs. Pusa Rascol
Dr. Mirinescu 12
Sector 6
Bucharest, Rumania
```

November 6, 1974

Mrs. Pusa Rascol
Dr. Mirinescu 12
Sector 6
Bucharest, Rumania

Dear Mrs. Rascol:

We here in the United States of America have heard of the trouble in your family, and wish you to know that you are not forgotten.

The members of our Prayer Group have remembered you and your family in our prayers, and will continue to pray that your husband will soon be returned to his family. Know that you are loved and remembered.

We hope you are well, and that your children are healthy and doing well.

Our prayers are offered for you and your family at this time.

Sincerely in Christ,
our Redeemer —

Praise Him always in all things!!

Wilma Helfen

Wilma Helfen
210 N. Indiana
Griffith, Ind.
United States of America

God's Faithfulness in Communist Romania

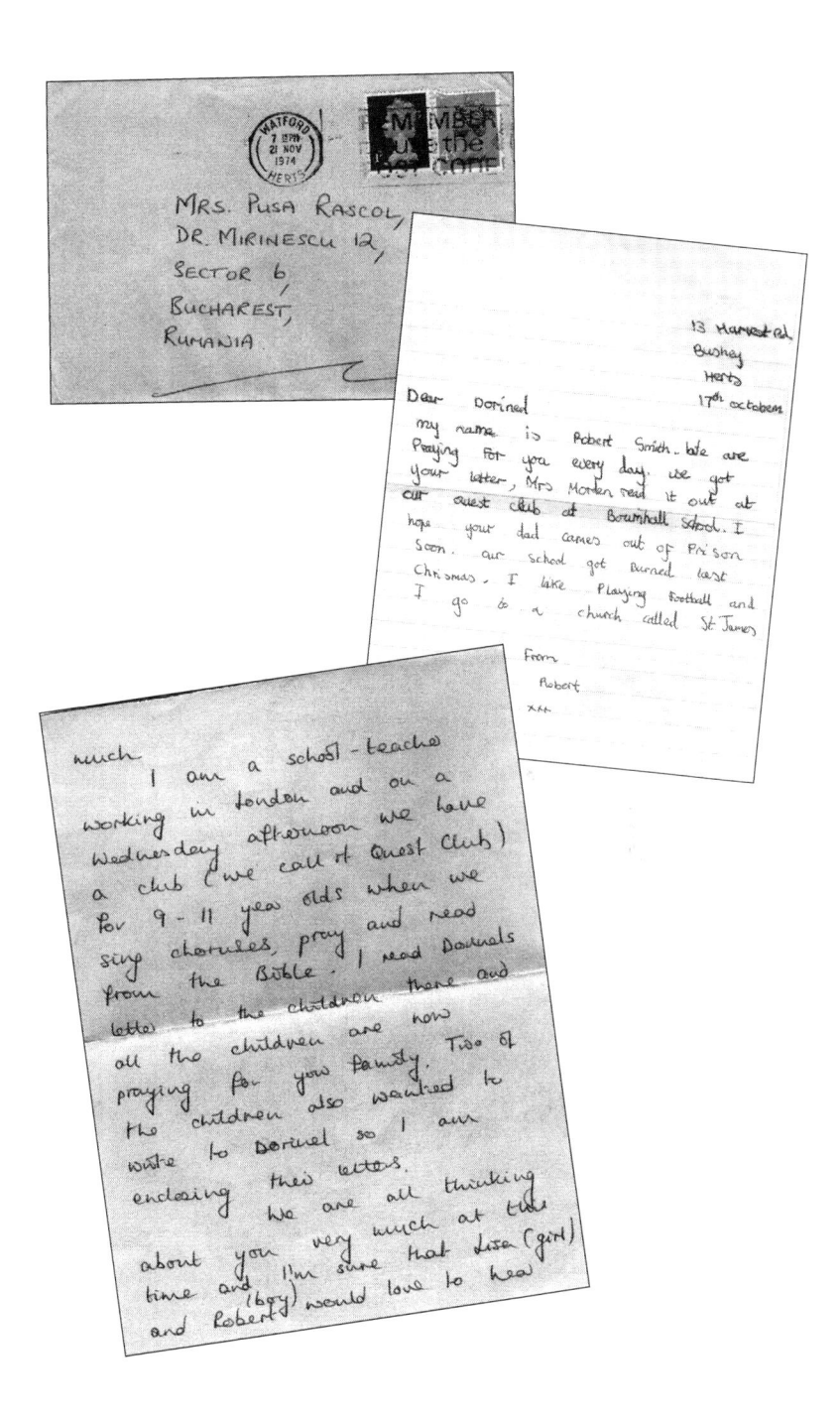

Envelope:

Mrs. Pusa Rascol,
Dr. Mirinescu 12,
Sector 6,
Bucharest,
Rumania

Postmark: Watford Herts, 21 Nov 1974

Letter 1:

13 Harvest Rd
Bushey
Herts
17th October

Dear Dorinel

My name is Robert Smith. We are praying for you every day. We got your letter, Mrs Morten read it out at our Quest club at Bournhall School. I hope your dad comes out of prison soon. Our school got burned last Christmas. I like playing football and I go to a church called St James

From
Robert
xxx

Letter 2:

...much. I am a school-teacher working in London and on a Wednesday afternoon we have a club (we call it Quest Club) for 9-11 year olds when we sing choruses, pray and read from the Bible. I read Dorinel's letter to the children there and all the children are now praying for your family. Two of the children also wanted to write to Dorinel so I am enclosing their letters.

We are all thinking about you very much at this time and I'm sure that Lisa (girl) and Robert (boy) would love to hear...